The New Genesis

Theology and the Genetic Revolution

Ronald Cole-Turner

Westminster/John Knox Press
Louisville, Kentucky

Book design by Peggy Claire Calhoun

First edition

This book is printed on recycled acid-free paper that meets the American National Standards Institute Z39.48 standard. ∞

Published by Westminster/John Knox Press
Louisville, Kentucky

PRINTED IN THE UNITED STATES OF AMERICA

9 8 7 6 5 4 3 2

Library of Congress Cataloging-in-Publication Data

Cole-Turner, Ronald, 1948–
    The new genesis : theology and the genetic revolution / by Ronald Cole-Turner. — 1st ed.
        p.   cm.
    Includes bibliographical references and index.
    ISBN 0-664-25406-3 (pbk. : acid-free paper)

    1. Genetic engineering—Religious aspects—Christianity. I. Title.
QH442.C64 1993   92-26564

Contents

Acknowledgments

Many people have helped in the preparation of this book. In 1985 I began research on theology and genetics as a fellow in the Coolidge Colloquium, and so I owe a great debt to William A. Coolidge, benefactor of the colloquium, as well as to Tony Stoneburner, director, and especially to Ian Barbour, an advisor for the colloquium that year.

I also want to thank Verlyn Barker, who is on the staff of the United Church Board for Homeland Ministries, for his invitation to chair two panels of the United Church of Christ on genetic engineering during the 1980s, and then for continuing to involve me in the activities of the United Church of Christ Working Group on Science and Technology since 1989. Many ideas in this book were developed in sessions that Verlyn sponsored, to which he contributed so much. In addition to Verlyn, I want to thank the members of that group, who often served as a sounding board for ideas; I am especially indebted to Olivia White and Brent Waters.

I also want to thank the late John Mangum of the Evangelical Lutheran Church in America for his bold vision of the mission of the church in a world pervasively transformed by science and technology, and for his encouragement of my contribution to that end.

Robert J. Russell and Ted Peters of the Center for Theology and the Natural Sciences also deserve my thanks. Many ideas I present here as my own were developed in conversations leading to a grant application made to the National Institutes of Health Office for Human Genome Research, which now funds our work through National Institutes of Health Grant HG00487-01.

I also thank the trustees and administrators of Memphis Theological Seminary for granting me a study leave during the second semester of 1989–1990, during which a significant portion of the manuscript was written.

Finally, those closest to the project deserve the most thanks, and so I thank my daughters, Sarah and Rachel, for their patience and for all that they have taught me about the inexplicable importance of biological continuity, and my wife, Rebecca, for her unwavering encouragement, for all the tasks she did in my stead, and most of all for her love.

Introduction

Genetic engineering is putting a new power into our hands. We are learning to revise the genetic code that is common to all living things on earth. With this power, we are claiming an unprecedented ability to alter nature.

Previous technologies affected nature, but always before we could assume that the genetic inheritance of species, including ourselves, lay largely beyond our reach. Genetic inheritance came to signify nature itself—nature as *natus, as that which is born*, inheriting inward principles that guide its development and set the limits, both physical and moral, of our technological alterations. Genetic engineering is unlike previous technologies: It redefines the meaning of *natus*. Earlier technologies altered nature primarily by altering environments outside living things. Genetic engineering will change nature by altering the genetic arrangement inside living things.

But to what end? How shall we alter the nature of the living things that surround us and upon which we depend? And how shall we alter our own human nature?

In the past, Western culture often turned to nature itself for guidance. It was believed that implicit in the nature of things is a moral framework to which human beings must consent. David Hume and G. E. Moore, however, questioned whether any moral obligation can be derived from nature. To infer an obligation from nature, or to reason from an "is" to an "ought," is to be guilty of an error of logic dubbed "the naturalist fallacy." In spite of this criticism, Western culture has generally been convinced that nature imposes some moral limit on human action. This conviction has experienced a rebirth with the rise of environmental ethics. Designating anything as "natural" also defines it as good, while the unnatural is morally suspect.

But can nature really guide a technology that has as its core project the alteration of nature? To think so would be to commit a naturalist fallacy of a new sort. In its traditional form, the alleged naturalist fallacy involved the assumption that there are moral obligations implicit in nature and binding on human behavior. Whether this is indeed a fallacy is, of course, a matter of continuing debate. But in its new form, occasioned by genetic engineering, the naturalist fallacy involves the assumption that whatever moral guidance may be implicit in nature is sufficient to guide not merely our acting upon nature but our transformation of nature. The fallacy here is twofold: It lies in thinking (1) that nature can disclose its own defects, toward the removal of which we human beings can then target our corrective technological interventions, and (2) that from nature *now* we can project a sufficiently clear notion of nature *as it should be* and thus aim our technological interventions accordingly.

Other problems also arise when we look to nature to supply the moral framework for our technology. In order to evaluate human technology in light of nature, we first have to distinguish the human from the natural. Without this distinction, everything human and everything technological is also natural and therefore morally permissible. Nature limits us only if we first see ourselves as an aberration within nature, as unnatural intruders within nature's innocence. But once we see ourselves as unnatural, we alienate ourselves from nature. What begins as a move toward nature becomes a move away from nature. Even though we are prompted by a desire to return to nature, we must first alienate ourselves from nature in order to put ourselves under the moral judgment of nature. Furthermore, any values we think we find in nature are more likely to be values that we are reading into nature. Unless we assume a naively realistic epistemology, we cannot hold that our idea of "the natural" literally corresponds to the way nature really is.

For all these reasons, we cannot look only to nature to guide our transformation of nature. With genetic engineering, genetic nature is itself malleable, an artifact of technology rather than its limit, and so now our alteration of nature needs *a guide beyond nature*. If there is any guide beyond nature by which our alterations of nature will be steered, it will of course arise within human culture. Through culture we stand out within nature. We create myths and stories, religions and technologies. We imagine ourselves as distinct within nature and claim for ourselves the right to direct the whole toward our ends. Through culture, we assign praise and blame, reward and punishment. We distinguish good from evil and normal from defective, and we imagine ideals of human health and happiness.

Our contemporary cultural life, however, is pluralistic, relativistic, even fragmented. No longer can we speak even of a Western culture. The moral relativity of cultural pluralism seems ill-equipped for the challenge posed by genetic engineering. Historic philosophies and religions no longer claim the allegiance of large communities. Into this relativistic morass comes genetic engineering, demanding what our cultures no longer seem capable of providing, namely, the power to guide, to envision the ideal, the good, the true, and the beautiful, and thus to define our presence on this planet.

For this reason, some argue that genetic engineering should be halted or greatly curtailed. They claim that until our wisdom catches up to our technological prowess, if it ever does, we would do better to leave nature to nature than to impose our passing fancies upon it (cf. Sinsheimer 1983; Rifkin 1983). We do not have the wisdom, these critics claim, to alter genetic inheritance.

There is good reason to fear the prospect of nature being altered according to the moral specifications of current cultural fads. As we develop the power to enhance certain genetic tendencies in our offspring, which tendencies will we enhance? Will we not be tempted to enhance those traits that are currently considered glamorous and well paid? Through genetic engineering, our culture's values are being edited into the genetic code. The guide beyond nature by which we will redefine nature may indeed turn out to be nothing but the latest cultural trend, an ill-considered whim of a myopic narcissism.

It is nonetheless encouraging to see that the developers of science are seeking the guidance of culture. For example, in the Human Genome Project, a major federal human genetics research project that has been funded by the United States government since the late 1980s, a portion of the research budget has been reserved for ethics research, including inquiry into the philosophical issues raised by human genetics. Commenting on recent trends to include cultural and religious resources in public deliberations on genetics, J. Robert Nelson notes:

> A remarkably free communication has developed between exponents of religious thought and genetic scientists (many of the latter, of course, being members of churches and synagogues). Theologians are now almost conventionally included in national conferences on genetics. . . .This unprecedented phenomenon represents a stark contrast to the separation of religion and science which many people have either taken for granted or have desired. It is a new era. (Nelson 1990, p. 47)

A recent survey of biology education notes a similar interest: Biology students are appealing to their instructors to address ethical questions, such as whether there are "ethical limits to what science and industry should produce in the way of new technologies" (Carter, Heppner, Saigo, et al. 1990, p. 681).

On the broader question of the environmental impact of technology, a group of prominent scientists appealed to the world's religious traditions for help in raising global concern about our impact on the planet. After pointing to the dangers caused by our disregard for nature, the scientists wrote, "We understand that what is regarded as sacred is more likely to be treated with care and respect. Our planetary home should be so regarded. Efforts to safeguard and cherish the environment need to be infused with a vision of the sacred" (Sagan, Bethe, Chandrasekhar, et al. 1990). These scientists apparently believed that science and technology alone could not provide the needed guidance and the motivation. "There is a vital role for both religion and science" (Sagan, Bethe, Chandrasekhar, et al. 1990). The role of science is to predict the consequences of our actions, while the role of religion is to guide us in choosing the right action. "We hope this Appeal will encourage a spirit of common cause and joint action to help preserve the Earth" (Sagan, Bethe, Chandrasekhar, et al. 1990).

As apprehensive as we might be of an unguided technological future, this fear alone will not permit us to claim the status of timeless truth for any artifact of culture, for any creed or text, for any tradition or way of life. Appeal to a religion must not become an escape from pluralism into tribalism or primitivism. At best, a religious tradition such as Christianity may be presumed to have the potential to be helpful now simply because it has proven itself helpful so often before.

In order to have the capability of speaking to our age, however, the Christian doctrines of the past need to absorb the insight of our age. Christianity has always done this. Its habit has been to import the best insights of every age. This tendency is now its strongest commendation in the present, for in Christianity we inherit the cumulative wisdom of two millennia of spiritual questioning and moral deliberation. It is not timeless but time-tested, seasoned by having proved itself a helpful guide in diverse times and places. When the insights of our age are added to this grand revisionary process known as Christian theology, the result is an intellectual and spiritual vision capable of speaking critically to our age.

Even as it draws upon the insight of our age, however, Christian theology should not forget its own perennial themes of creation and redemption, sin and grace, incarnation and transfiguration. These enduring themes give Christianity its critical edge. They should not be surrendered; however, preserving them requires that we restate them. For example, it will be argued later that Christianity's idea of a fall into sin needs to be thoroughly restated, but that its core claim—that nature is good but disordered—must be preserved. In earlier times, Christians could express this belief by speaking of the historic fall of the first two human beings, Adam and Eve, just a few thousand years ago. This explanation of the origin of disorder is no longer plausible or illuminating. Even so, the Christian conviction that there is a moral disorder that pervades the creation is a provocative idea, for it suggests a way in which we might think about a technology such as genetic engineering. If such a moral disorder exists in nature, and if God is understood to be at work creatively and redemptively resolving that disorder, and if we recognize ourselves as invited by God to participate in that creative and redemptive work, then we can see our technology, especially our genetic engineering, as a partnership with God in the expanding and redeeming of nature.

Within this theological context, genetic engineering is seen as a legitimate human activity. In fact, genetic engineering is encouraged as a Christian calling or vocation, a work to which we are summoned by God and through which we participate in the work of God. For this reason, however, genetic engineering is sharply restrained and redirected. It is not to be used for self-indulgent or destructive ends, to amass power, or to increase the dependence of the technologically poor upon the technologically rich. On the contrary, genetic engineering is to be used in ways that are consistent with the activity of God the Creator and Redeemer. Its goals should be to heal, to restore, to conserve, and to explore.

Urging greater interaction between theology and science, Nobel physicist Charles Townes has commented, "How important it is for those of us who are scientifically or technically skilled to understand and participate in God's purposes. How important it is for those whose special role it is to study religion to also understand the context, the problems, and the challenges of mankind's creative scientific future!" (C. Townes 1988, p. 16). The interchange that Townes envisions between theology and the scientific fields is a two-way street. Theology has a great deal to learn from the sciences, especially now from the science of human genetics. But theology also has a uniquely important role to play in constructing the moral framework that will guide our scientific research and our technological transformations. When traffic flows both ways on the street connecting science and technology, then the hope expressed by Jürgen Moltmann may come to pass, that "theology and the sciences will arrive together at the ecological awareness of the world" (Moltmann 1985, p. 34).

Two goals, therefore, have guided the writing of this book. This study is intended as a contribution to Christian theology's understanding of science and technology, especially in the areas of genetics and genetic engineering. But it is also hoped that through this study, Christian theology will become more adequate to the challenge that scientists themselves are putting to it, namely, to help in steering the future of our technologically advanced civilization.

Over a century ago, the popular theologian Horace Bushnell wrote:

> It has been my endeavor to put honor on faith—to restore, if possible, the genuine, apostolic faith. I have even wished, shall I dare to say, hoped, that I might do something to inaugurate that faith in the field of modern science, and claim for it there that respect to which, in the sublimity of its reasons, it is entitled. And great will be the day when faith, laying hold of science and rising into intellectual majesty with it, is acknowledged in the glorious sisterhood of a common purpose, and both lead in the realms they occupy, reconciled to God, cleared of the disorders and woes of sin, to set them in that final unity which represents the eternal Headship of Christ. (Bushnell 1903 [1858], p. 510)

Little could Bushnell have anticipated how urgent this task would become.

1

The Age of Genetic Engineering

Genetic engineering is so new and developing with such speed that it might transform us as a species before we notice what has occurred. Yet we must comprehend this technology if we are to have any hope of guiding it. If we are to ask about the religious significance of genetic engineering, we must first understand what genetic engineering is and what some of its major uses are. Therefore, we will review the development of this technology (see Table 1.1), noting the wide range of its applications and anticipating future directions in research.

Genetics and Genetic Engineering

About ten thousand years ago, some of our ancestors gradually changed from hunter-gatherers to sedentary farmers. Part of agriculture is selective breeding, the slow process by which plants and animals are domesticated. By planting the best seeds or by breeding the best animals, better varieties of grains, vegetables, fruits, and livestock were developed. In this way, human beings engineered or acted technologically upon the genes of other species. In recent centuries, breeders became highly skilled in achieving specific results within a short period of time. These results were achieved without the benefit of our contemporary scientific understanding of genetics.

The study of genetics had its historic start in the pioneering scientific work of Gregor Mendel (1822–1884). His laborious experiments with pea plants demonstrated that there are units of hereditary information passed through seeds from parent plants to offspring. Sometimes these units of information are unexpressed in a generation, but eventually they are expressed with predictable regularity. These units of information are known to us as genes.

Mendel's work demonstrated that units of information are transferred from parent plants to offspring, but just what are these informational units or genes? What is their chemical structure? How can chemicals encode information? How can they repeat this information and pass it on to future generations? And how do they communicate their information to the cell that contains them? Mendel's discovery raised these intriguing questions for modern molecular biology and genetics.

About the time of Mendel's work, the molecule deoxyribonucleic acid (DNA) was isolated by Friedrich Miescher. During the 1940s scientists identified DNA as the chemical responsible for Mendel's units of genetic information—that is, that genes are made of DNA. Through X-ray crystallography it was learned that DNA has the structure of a double helix. In 1953 Francis Crick and James Watson described how the strands of the DNA molecule are arranged in a double helix, in such a way that DNA can, first, replicate itself faithfully and, second, carry information. Along the DNA strand, chemical patterns act like the letters of a code, conveying genetic instructions for the building of the cell.

By 1966 scientists were able to give a complete description of the chemical elements of the genetic alphabet. The DNA molecule, which is huge by molecular standards, is composed of four groups of chemicals, repeated over and over in different sequences along the twined strands of the molecule. These four chemicals are bases (as opposed to acids) and are abbreviated A, G, T, and C (for adenine, guanine, thymine, and cytosine). By their sequence, these bases code the information needed to produce the twenty amino acids that are the building blocks of proteins. Proteins, in turn, form the structure of the cell, the fundamental organizational unit of life.

The four bases always occur in pairs. Opposite every A on one strand is a T on the other strand, and for every G there is a matching C on the other strand. These pairs of A–T or C– G can become separated, like the two sides of a zipper. Each side of the opened DNA "zipper" then acts as a template: The unpaired bases of the split strands attract their complementary bases, loose in the cell nucleus; this forms, for each opened side of the double helix, an exact replica of its opposite side. In this way, DNA copies itself every time a cell divides. This ability of DNA to replicate is basic to all living things, separating them from the nonliving.

Early in the 1970s scientists learned how certain chemicals found in the cell can cut a DNA chain. These chemicals, called *restriction enzymes*, cut through the double DNA strand at a precise spot in the sequence. Another enzyme, a ligase, reattaches DNA fragments. Once they knew how these enzymes worked, researchers were able to use the enzymes to insert new genetic material into bacterial DNA. After isolating plasmids, or small circles of DNA in bacterial cells, they cut the plasmid DNA circle with a restriction enzyme, making a strand. Then they attached "foreign" DNA—that is, DNA from another kind of organism—to one end of the plasmid DNA. The plasmid DNA was reconnected to form a circle and then reinserted into the bacteria cell, which would recommence reproduction. Each time the cell divided, the plasmid replicated or copied itself, together with the inserted foreign DNA. This was the beginning of recombinant DNA technology. DNA from two sources had been joined, and it produced copies of itself in its modified, hybrid form.

Quickly, the scientific community began to theorize about applications.

If it was possible to insert new genes into organisms, all kinds of therapeutic and agricultural applications were possible. But just as quickly, alarming dangers became evident to many scientists. A letter appearing simultaneously in *Nature* and *Science* and signed by eleven of the leading researchers stated, "Although such experiments are likely to facilitate the solution of important theoretical and practical biological problems, they would also result in the creation of novel types of infectuous DNA elements whose biological properties cannot be completely predicted in advance" (Berg 1974, p. 303).

The letter called for a moratorium on virtually all lines of recombinant DNA research. It asked the National Institutes of Health (NIH) to form an advisory committee and to begin preparing guidelines for future work. Finally, the letter called for an international meeting "to review scientific progress in this area and to further discuss appropriate ways to deal with the potential biohazards of recombinant DNA molecules" (Berg 1974, p. 303).

This meeting took place in the winter of 1975, and soon the NIH began the process of developing guidelines for research. Throughout the remainder of the 1970s, however, there were many misgivings about the risks of genetic engineering. Scientists themselves voiced their concerns, and the wider public (including the religious communities) became involved in the debate.

Also in 1975 C. Milstein and G. Kohler, working in Cambridge, England, fused two types of cells together. One of the cells was a lymphocyte, which can produce antibodies capable of identifying and fighting disease. The other cell was a cancer cell, which can multiply indefinitely. By fusing these two cells, the capabilities of each were transferred to a new kind of cell, called a *hybridoma*. The hybridoma cell multiplies and produces a very specific antibody, known as a monoclonal antibody. Milstein and Kohler suggested to the British government that their technique be patented. When they received no response, they published their findings, and the technique became widely adopted in laboratories around the world (Milstein and Kohler 1975, p. 495; *Science* 1982, p. 1074). Today it is used to produce a wide variety of diagnostic and therapeutic products.

The brisk pace of discovery since the early 1970s has astounded observers, even those who have been at its center. Again and again, predicted schedules for future research were too generous with time. By the late 1980s, genetic engineering was applied widely to agriculture and to human health.

Before discussing these recent and foreseeable applications, we should settle on definitions of "gene," "recombinant DNA," and "genetic engineering." The definitions we will use are taken from a President's Commission (1982). The gene is defined as "the hereditary unit, such as a segment of DNA coding for a specific protein" (President's

Commission 1982, p. 91). *Recombinant DNA* is defined as "the hybrid DNA produced by joining pieces of DNA from different sources" (President's Commission 1982, p. 92). This was first accomplished by researchers in the early 1970s. *Genetic engineering* refers to the various techniques (including cell fusion) by which recombinant DNA can be produced. The report defines it as "a wide range of techniques by which scientists can add genetically determined characteristics to cells that would not otherwise have possessed them" (President's Commission 1982, p. 8). Later, the report identifies genetic engineering as "the directed manipulation of the genetic material itself" (President's Commission 1982, p. 92).

When the topic of genetic engineering arises, many related topics often arise too. These other topics range from in vitro fertilization to cloning to genetic screening. We will not include them here as genetic engineering. However, since these techniques are heavily dependent upon developments in genetic engineering, we will refer to them in our discussion.

Emerging Developments

Genetic engineering has widely diverse applications. Research is underway to apply its techniques to forestry, mining, environmental concerns, and waste treatment projects. Agriculture and human health, however, will inevitably be the major areas for the application of genetic engineering. In the following paragraphs, we will list recent and foreseeable uses of genetic engineering, beginning with agriculture and human health, and then moving to other areas of research.

Agricultural Animals

In the early 1980s experiments with mice led to the successful introduction of a rat growth hormone gene into the DNA of mice (Palmiter, Brinster, and Hammer, 1982). The rat gene was introduced into the mouse embryo, and so it was replicated each time the mouse's cells divided. This meant it was present in the mouse's sex cells and transmitted to its offspring, producing a race of fast-growing mice. These mice are then referred to as *transgenic,* since their genome contains a gene from another species.

This experiment with mice set off a wave of excitement. If mice could grow larger more quickly, why not farm animals? Many experiments are being conducted, but "the extrapolation of this technology from mice to livestock was not as simple and straightforwards as some imagined it would be" (Womack 1987, 66). For example, when researchers attempted to use genetic engineering to produce leaner, faster-growing pigs, they were unsuccessful, largely because it is difficult to get the growth hormone gene to express itself without upsetting the expression of other genes. In a United States Department of Agriculture study of pigs, "eight of fourteen transgenic animals studied died before 90 days of age and there were significant problems of lethargy, muscle weakness, uncoordination, lack of libido, and susceptibility to stress in these transgenic pigs" (Lamming 1988, p. 19; cf. Marx 1988a, p. 33). Undoubtedly, this research will continue, despite apprehensiveness about the true desirability of the intended result. According to one observer, among researchers "there is a widespread fear that such techniques [leading to increased growth rates] could exacerbate food surpluses and put small farmers out of business" (Lamming 1988, p. 19). A recent summary of the application of genetic engineering to farm animals ended with this prediction: "The continued extrapolation of these techniques to farm animals will ultimately result in more productive and healthier livestock" (Pursel, Pinkert, Miller, et al. 1989, p. 1287). Not only could a growth hormone gene be transferred, but so could genes conferring resistance to disease, increased milk production, or increased protein level in the meat. For example, research is underway to confer to cattle a genetic resistance to trypanosomiasis or sleeping sickness, which is carried to dairy cattle in Africa by the tsetse fly (Roberts 1990a, p. 552).

Another research strategy is to transfer a human gene that produces a vital human protein to a domesticated animal. For example, a human gene inserted in sheep will produce a "human" protein in the sheep's mammary glands, and the protein can be extracted from the milk (Marx 1988a, p. 32). This is a particularly attractive strategy for synthesizing proteins, such as blood-clotting enzymes, that cannot be readily synthesized by altered microorganisms (Pursel, Pinkert, Miller, et al. 1989, p. 1281). By 1986 researchers produced transgenic sheep that transmitted the inserted human gene to their offspring, while the ewes secreted the desired human proteins in their milk (Cherfas 1990, p. 125). This demonstrates "that transgenic animals may soon revolutionize the supply of therapeutic compounds" (Cherfas 1990, p. 126).

In 1987 the United States Patent Office approved a patent application for a transgenic animal, stating that the office would not reject applications simply because they involved animals. The patented animal, a mouse, carries a human oncogene (a gene the leads to cancer). This makes the mouse a highly valuable cancer research tool, and these mice currently sell for about fifty dollars each. However, in the wake of the announcement from the Patent Office, there was such a public expression of concern that the Patent Office had not, as of the spring of 1989, accepted any more applications for transgenic animals, despite the fact that forty-four such applications were pending (Ezzell 1989, p. 366).

More recently, attempts have been made to produce a genetic map of various agricultural animals. (Genetic mapping is the "determining of the relative locations of different genes on a given chromosome" [President's Commission 1982, p. 91].) This will give researchers the knowledge of where, in the genetic material, genes responsible for certain traits are located. Knowing this, researchers will be able to screen embryos for the presence of certain genes that will be expressed as desirable traits. "The biggest obstacle is that the traits that matter, like fat deposition or milk production, are controlled not by one gene but by many" (Roberts 1990a, p. 550). Looking for these genes one at a time would be too expensive. But if the entire genome of dairy cattle is understood, researchers may be able to determine which genes are responsible for milk production.

Genetic mapping and screening allows researchers to select embryos, in the earliest stages of their development, based on the desirability of the traits the mature animal would have. Embryos can be recovered (without surgery) from cows that have been made to superovulate through the use of fertility drugs and transferred to other cows who may be less desirable genetically. This selection "may very well come to be recognized as genetic engineering's major contribution to animal agriculture" (Womack 1987, p. 68). In addition, embryos can be split before implantation, producing twins or clones.

Agricultural Plants

Researchers are using genetic engineering with agricultural plants, hoping to produce better protein content, resistance to disease or other environmental stresses, ability to self-fertilize or to utilize fertilizer more efficiently, and maintenance of diverse genetic resources. These advances would permit agriculture that is less reliant on toxic chemicals, fertilizers, irrigation, and energy resources.

Plants such as rice and cereal grains make up over half the world's food. One problem with them as food sources (aside from our vulnerability in being dependent upon so few species) is that they do not produce the whole range of proteins needed in the human diet. As much as 70 percent of the human population depends on these plants for the bulk of its protein. Since proteins are produced according to genetic instructions, researchers are hopeful that plants may be altered genetically to produce the full range of needed proteins.

Another genetic engineering research strategy has been to find ways to make plants more resistant to environmental stresses, such as frost, drought, and high salt content in the soil. Researchers have altered a type of bacteria, making it capable of retarding frost on strawberry and potato plants (Ezzell 1987, p. 90). Some success has been achieved in developing strains of cotton and tomatoes that can be irrigated with seawater (Gibbons 1990a, p. 963).

Among agricultural plants, legumes (for example, soybeans) have the ability to be partly self-fertilizing by fixing nitrogen in the soil. Actually, the plants' roots serve as the host to bacteria that do the nitrogen fixing. A widespread hope is that someday genetic engineering will give this nitrogen-fixing ability to other plants, thereby cutting the need for fertilizers substantially. Already for several decades, farmers planting legumes have used seeds that are treated with the nitrogen-fixing bacteria. This increases the amount of nitrogen left in the soil. Recently, researchers altered this type of bacteria, giving it extra copies of the gene responsible for the nitrogen. This increased the nitrogen fixation even further, but only in plants that already serve as host to the bacteria (Ezzell 1987, p. 90).

Researchers have also succeeded in introducing traits for disease resistance into plants. Others have introduced herbicide resistance, allowing farmers to use herbicides to control all but the desired plant (Lamb and Fitzmaurice 1986, p. 414).

In the future, genetically altered plants may provide an increasing amount of chemical raw material for chemical engineering, somewhat replacing coal and oil in this regard. In addition, research is now underway to alter plants so they will produce mammalian proteins. If successful, plants may be an expanded source of medical products. The major agricultural application of genetic engineering, however, will be to enhance the quality and quantity of food produced by the plants. "In view of the rapid progress that is being made, it is likely that all major . . . crop species will be amenable to improvement by genetic engineering within the next few years" (Gasson and Fraley 1989, p. 1293).

Pharmaceuticals

One of the most attractive applications of genetic engineering is in the pharmaceutical industry. Genes are the basis for the production of the proteins upon which the human body depends. In some individuals, however, a gene may be missing or misfunctioning, and so an essential protein or hormone may not be produced. A shortage of insulin (diabetes) or of growth hormone (dwarfism) can have serious health implications. Researchers have taken the human gene for insulin, inserted it into bacteria, and let the bacteria multiply. The altered bacteria produce human insulin, which can be used to treat diabetics. Research is underway to produce many other similar products by inserting human genes into bacteria or into domesticated animals or plants.

Vaccines

First developed by the English physician Edward Jenner in the 1790s, vaccines prompt the body's immune system to fight off diseases such as smallpox and polio. Since Jenner's revolutionary work, only twelve vaccines have been developed against human diseases. However, because of genetic engineering, researchers are confident that several important vaccines will be developed in the future. The most widely known vaccine research using genetic engineering techniques is the development of a vaccine for acquired immune deficiency syndrome

(AIDS). Another vaccine in development is for malaria, which has evaded other means of control and is now undergoing a resurgence in some parts of the world. Currently, there are 200–300 million cases per year and over 2 billion people live in infected areas. Research is proceeding more slowly than first expected, but researchers remain optimistic about eventual success "even though a highly effective, long-lasting, multivalent vaccine against malaria will probably not be available in [the] next few years" (S. Hoffman, Nussenzweig, Sadoff, et al., 1991, p. 521; cf. Moss 1991). Another disease being extensively researched is sleeping sickness, which is transmitted by the tsetse fly throughout central Africa. As with malaria, the disease is difficult to control because it has evolved clever means of protecting itself (Kolata 1984). This means that even with genetic engineering, a vaccine for the disease will be difficult and risky to produce. Unfortunately, since vaccines for malaria and sleeping sickness are mostly needed in the world's poor nations, there is little market incentive for their development.

Mapping the Human Genome

In any species, the individuals share a basic genetic structure. Already, researchers know a great deal about the location of various genes within the human genome. However, since the late 1980s a massive project has been underway to map the entire human genome. When the Human Genome Project is completed, the chromosomal location of every human gene will be known. This work will be done in several countries.

In the course of the project, discoveries of disease-linked genes have been reported with increasing frequency, sometimes simultaneously by researchers working independently, as in the case of the gene for neurofibromatosis type 1 (Roberts 1990c, pp. 236–37) and the discovery of the site of the fragile X syndrome mutation (Hoffman 1991).

Many human diseases have a genetic basis that lies in more than one gene. For example, various forms of cancer, heart disease, high blood pressure, and mental disorders such as schizophrenia are influenced by several genes interacting with one another and with environmental factors such as diet. These diseases affect many more people than do single-gene (or Mendelian) disorders such as sickle cell anemia or cystic fibrosis. It is hoped that the Human Genome Project will make research into these multigenetic diseases more successful (Marx 1990, p. 1542).

The Human Genome Project raises complex philosophical and ethical issues. The director of the project for the National Institutes of Health, James Watson, described the objective of the project as the attempt "to find out what being human is" (*Science* 1989a, p. 167). In Europe, environmental activists (the Greens) have raised criticisms. A Green representative to the European Community Parliament stated, "We are playing with the very substance of humankind and human dignity"

(Dickson 1989, p. 599). In the United States and in Europe, the project will include funding for studies into its ethical and social implications.

Genetic Screening and Diagnosis

A variety of techniques make it possible to detect the presence of particular genes, such as those responsible for genetic diseases. DNA "probes," for example, can bind to specific genetic sequences and signal their location through radioactivity or fluorescence. Such probes have been developed for a large number of human genetic disorders, as well as to identify viruses and bacteria with (for example) resistance to drugs. Monoclonal antibodies, themselves products of genetic engineering, can also be used to reveal the presence of disease.

In the next decade or so these screening techniques will directly affect more people than will any other health application of genetic engineering. Already, certain forms of genetic screening are becoming routine. Prenatal screening for a wide range of defects is now possible. As progress is made with efforts to map the human genome, more genetic defects will be detectable. Newer techniques, which require a smaller sample of fetal DNA, permit testing earlier in the pregnancy. In 1989 it was announced in Britain and in Australia that in cases of in vitro fertilization, zygotes are screened prior to their insertion into the mother's uterus. The embryo is allowed to divide to four or more cells, and one of these cells is removed without the others being damaged. The DNA from the removed cell is then screened for defects (Hastings Center 1989, p. 48). If defects are found, then the embryo is not implanted. In 1990 a center in Britain announced that they had used in vitro fertilization and then screened embryos for sex. This was done for couples at risk for conceiving a son with an X-linked genetic disease (Handyside, Kontogianni, Hardy, et al. 1990). In the same year, researchers succeeded in screening unfertilized eggs for one of the cystic fibrosis mutations. This technique extended the screening process backward in time from preimplantation to preconception. The researchers claim that "this study demonstrates the feasibility of preconception and preimplantation diagnosis for couples who carry" a particular cystic fibrosis mutation (Strom, Verlinsky, Milayeva, et al. 1990, p. 307).

With in utero conception, genetic testing can lead to the diagnosis of a genetic defect. A few genetic defects can be treated in utero, but most cannot. For those defects that cannot be treated, the only other medical intervention is abortion. This raises complex questions about whether parents want the information that results from prenatal screening and how they will be helped in acting upon it.

An additional concern is whether prenatal diagnosis is being used for sex selection. Genetic screening, as well as other forms of prenatal diagnosis such as ultrasound, indicates the sex of the fetus. Dorothy Wertz and John Fletcher argue that since there is evidence to indicate that parents are using this information to selectively abort a fetus whose sex they do not want, "examining the ethical arguments on sex selection through prenatal diagnosis and their implications for social policy is now an urgent task" (Wertz and Fletcher 1989). It is believed that abortion for sex selection is particularly common in India because of strong cultural pressures to have a son instead of a daughter.

Genetic Fingerprinting

Genetic screening techniques have recently been applied to the science of forensics. In 1988 the Federal Bureau of Investigation (FBI) established a laboratory to keep genetic records of criminals, much as fingerprint records are kept. Several states, particularly California, are in the process of setting up laboratories at the state level, with the prospect of the FBI providing national coordination (*New York Times* 1989). Genetic analysis of a trace amount of tissue (including hair or semen) can link the tissue with its donor, although the degree of reliability of the linkage has been challenged (Lewontin and Hartl 1991; cf. Chakraborty and Kidd 1991). At a crime scene, tissue is often left even when fingerprints are not. And unlike fingerprints, genetic analysis of a sample of a child's cells can be used to identify the parents. This technique is already being used to establish paternity or to identify a rapist. (*Science* 1988). Eventually it may be possible to draw a genetic composite (hair color, height, skin color, even facial features) from genetic analysis.

Somatic Cell Gene Therapy

About six thousand human diseases are based on single genetic defects. Traditional medicine can treat some of these, but no cure is possible. Somatic cell gene therapy will make it possible to correct the genetic defect in the specific tissues that the disease affects. Since gene therapy involves altering the genes in some of the cells of a patient, its procedures are complex, and the approval process has been long, even tortuous. After years of public debate, approval was given in 1989 for clinical trials of gene therapy techniques (Culliton 1989, p. 913), and in 1990 gene therapy itself began.

Gene therapy is potentially applicable to a wide range of genetic diseases, from bone marrow disorders to cystic fibrosis to diseases affecting the liver. Somatic cell gene therapy with rabbits was successful in treating familial hypercholesterolemia. Researchers hope that the techniques can be adapted to treat a number of inherited liver diseases in human patients (Roberts 1988b). In addition, gene therapy may be applicable to genetic diseases of the central nervous system, such as Lesch-Nyhan disease (Friedmann 1989, p. 1278). Gene therapy also offers techniques applicable to cancer and perhaps to infectious diseases. Research is currently underway to overcome the greatest technical problem of gene therapy, namely, how to transfer new genetic material effectively into the cells of a patient. For example, two teams independently discovered techniques to treat the cystic fibrosis defect in cells grown in a culture in a laboratory. In the cell culture, the defect that causes cystic fibrosis was corrected. The problem now is to correct the defect in the lungs of the cystic fibrosis patient (Roberts 1990b). Also in 1990, researchers successfully used an adenovirus, which naturally infects lung cells, as the carrier for transferring a human gene to the lungs of rats (Rosenfeld, Siegfried, Yoshimura, et al. 1991, pp. 431–34). This work increases significantly the potential use of gene therapy for cystic fibrosis and emphysema.

Any gene therapy attempted in the foreseeable future must not affect the sex cells of the patient. If the sex cells were affected, the genetic alteration might be transmitted to the patient's offspring, and to their offspring indefinitely. United States federal guidelines say that any proposed therapy must avoid altering the germline cells and affect somatic or body cells only.

Human Germline Therapy

Some genetic diseases affect many areas of the body. In such cases, somatic cell gene therapy will probably never be practical. An alternative would be to replace the defective gene when the individual consists of only one cell, as a fertilized egg or zygote. If successful, this would mean that the whole body would contain the correct gene. But it would also enter the germline and be passed to the individual's offspring.

Similar experiments have been conducted with animals, with some success but with numerous difficulties too. A great number of technical obstacles remain before any responsible researcher would propose an experiment with human zygotes. It is difficult to perform the therapy without harming a zygote. Furthermore, this approach to therapy inevitably raises issues of eugenics. By what social standard are "defective" genes determined to be defective? And if it is possible to replace defective genes, is it not also possible to replace normal genes with enhanced genes (for greater athletic ability or intelligence)? Inevitably, as the techniques improve, the question of human germline therapy will become an urgent public issue. In 1991 the National Institutes of Health announced the formation of a panel to discuss the ethical questions of human germline alterations *(Science* 1991a, p. 841).

If it becomes possible to remove and replace a *defective* gene, it will probably also be possible to remove a normal gene and replace it with one that is thought to be superior. Perhaps in the next century, these procedures will be technically feasible. It may even be possible, some day, to enhance intelligence or to diminish aggression. This would require changing a large number of genes. Before these procedures become technically feasible, widespread discussion should occur about the advisability of attempting to enhance the genetic inheritance of our offspring.

Behavioral Genetics

Research into the genetic basis of human behavior takes two broad forms, quantitative and molecular. In quantitative research, twins or siblings are compared for similarities in their behavior or attitudes. Researchers are interested in statistical correlations, not in specific genes. In molecular genetics, on the other hand, specific genes are identified as contributing to certain behaviors such as alcoholism. Until the 1980s quantitative research was the only possible approach to the genetics of behavior. Recent developments in genetic engineering and the rapid expansion of knowledge of the human genome have made it possible for researchers to look for specific genes that lie at the basis of behavior.

In thinking about quantitative behavioral genetics, it is important to recall that domesticated animals have been bred for their behavior as much as for their size or productivity. Dogs, especially, have been bred for their trainability for certain tasks such as herding or hunting. Although humans have not been bred for behavior, we still have genes that affect our behavior.

Quantitative behavioral genetics has attempted to determine the extent to which our behavior is attributable to our genes. By comparing identical and fraternal twins, both those raised together and those who were adopted separately, researchers have been able to determine that genes account for approximately 50 percent of the observed variation in complex traits such as intelligence (IQ) or personality type. Summarizing recent research, Robert Plomin comments, "The heritability of IQ scores is between 30 and 70%. Nonetheless, even if the heritability of IQ scores is at the bottom of this range, it is a remarkable finding. To account for 30% of the variance of anything as complex as IQ scores is a remarkable achievement" (Plomin 1990, p. 185). Summarizing data from the Minnesota Study of Twins Reared Apart, Thomas Bouchard notes that "about 70% of the observed variation in IQ in this population can be attributed to genetic variation" (Bouchard, Lykken, and McGue 1990, p. 227). Since the population in the study was more homogeneous than that of the general society, the 70% correlation cannot be extrapolated without adjustment. "Moreover, these findings do not imply that traits like IQ cannot be enhanced" (Bouchard, Lykken, and McGue 1990, p. 227).

Studies also indicate that personality traits are genetically influenced. Summarizing several studies, Plomin notes, "Four twins studies in four countries involving over 30,000 pairs of twins yield heritability estimates of about 50% for neuroticism and extraversion" (Plomin 1990, p. 185). Bouchard et al. found that genetic inheritance accounts for 49% of the variation in religiosity or the tendency to be religious (Bouchard et al. 1990, p. 226).

Studies of identical twins are beginning to claim that genetic heredity partly explains a wide range of human behaviors and traits. One recent study linked obesity to genetics (Bouchard, Tremblay, and Després 1990). Late in 1991 researchers announced that they had found evidence of a link between genetic inheritance and homosexuality. A study of 56 pairs of identical twins, in which one of each pair was openly homosexual, indicated that 29 (or 52%) of the twin brothers were also homosexual. By comparison, only 12 of the fraternal twin brothers of 54 homosexual men were themselves homosexual, and only 6 nontwin brothers of 57 homosexual men were homosexual. This suggests that genetic heredity plays an important role in sexual orientation (Bailey and Pillard 1991). There is little doubt that additional studies will reexamine this early conclusion.

When we think about how genes work, we usually think of single-gene disorders that follow simple Mendelian rules. There are more than six thousand human genetic diseases that are Mendelian or single-gene disorders. Behavior, however, is probably influenced by many genes, each contributing in a small way. This is probably why behavior and personality traits are found in a continuum of variability, unlike single-gene disorders that are either present or absent. Intelligence, for example, is expressed as a score, not as a simple yes/no diagnosis.

If it is true that the genetic basis for behavior involves many genes, will it ever be possible to identify which genes contribute to a particular behavior? Will it be possible to move from quantitative behavioral genetics to molecular behavioral genetics? Developing the relevant genetics technology will make the search easier. So will the data base of the human genome that will be generated as a result of the Human Genome Program. "One of the many benefits of this project will be the identification of more markers and genes that might play a role in genetic variation of behavior" (Plomin 1990, p. 187). In 1991 the National Institutes of Health funded research to look for specific genes that play a role in behavior *(Science* 1991b, p. 1352). In the future, it will very likely be discovered that certain combinations of several specific genes contribute to many behavioral or personality traits.

In 1990 a team of researchers reported finding a specific gene that contributed to alcoholism (Blum, Noble, Sheridan, et al. 1990). This finding was not confirmed by a subsequent study (Bolos, Dean, Lucas-Derse, et al. 1990). So complex is the question of the causes of alcoholism that the National Institute on Alcohol Abuse and Alcoholism has funded a major study of the genetic, social, and psychological factors associated with the disease (Holden 1991b, pp. 163–64). Researchers involved in the study hold differing views on whether there are specific genes that contribute to some forms of alcoholism. For example, the principal investigator, Henri Bergleiter, suspects that "the same biological core of anomalies" lies at the base of a wide range of addictions (quoted by Holden 1991b, p. 164). Such complex genetic studies are possible because of advanced computerized techniques and because of expanded knowledge of the human genome.

Technical Advances

Technical advances in genetic engineering made in the late 1980s mean that future work will proceed at an even faster pace. For example, the new technique of *homologous recombination*, known more popularly as *gene targeting*, allows scientists to be much more precise in their efforts. This increases the speed and, in the case of future human somatic cell gene therapy, the feasibility and moral acceptability of genetic therapy. Describing this new technique, Mario Capecchi comments, "The potential now exists for modifying any gene, in a defined manner, in any species from which functional ES cells [pluripotent, embryo-derived stem cells] can be obtained" (Capecchi 1989a, p. 1288). Such ES cells can be obtained from a widening number of mammals. Plant cells from anywhere in the plant are typically pluripotent, or capable of generating a whole plant. According to Paul Berg, before this new technique, "the best we could do is put a gene into cells and stand back and pray" (quoted in Marx 1988b, p. 191). Now it is possible to target the inserted gene to an exact site in the genome. "The power of gene targeting resides in the ability of the experimenter to precisely choose both the gene to be modified and the specific change to be introduced" (Capecchi 1989a, p. 1292).

The *polymerase chain reaction* (PCR), a technique developed in the mid-1980s, permits researchers to make millions of copies of a section of DNA within the space of hours. This permits a wide range of genetic engineering applications that would not be feasible otherwise (Erlich, Gelfand, and Sninsky 1991). Another technical advance allows researchers to cut very long sections of DNA at precisely one location. This ability is particularly helpful when dealing with entire chromosomes and when attempting a genome map (Roberts 1990d).

Conclusions

A major goal of the federal Human Genome Project is to stimulate technical advances. It is altogether likely that technical advances in genetic engineering will continue in the future. In addition, the relationship between genes and proteins is becoming much more clearly understood. This means that genetic engineering will become even faster and more powerful, perhaps becoming capable not only of moving genes from one organism to another but also of custom-designing genes to build specific proteins. As these technical advances in genetics occur, they will raise new and challenging questions about what it is to be human and what role we should have in nature.

Table 1.1 Developments in Genetics

1865   Gregor Mendel describes statistical patterns of inheritance in peas.

1869   Friedrich Miescher discovers deoxyribonucleic acid (DNA) and later isolates it.

1943   Oswald T. Avery, Colin MacLeod, and Maclyn McCarty argue that DNA is the vehicle of inheritance, and Avery conjectures that it can be manipulated.

1953   James D. Watson and Francis H. Crick describe the double-helical structure of DNA, showing how it can replicate and carry information.

1960   The genetic messenger RNA is discovered.

1965   Rollin D. Hotchkiss coins the phrase "genetic engineering" (Hotchkiss 1965).

1966   Scientists describe the complete genetic code.

1967   The enzyme ligase that joins DNA strands is isolated.

1970   A restriction enzyme that cuts DNA at a specific site is discovered.

1972   Paul Berg cuts DNA with a restriction enzyme and joins it with ligase—this is the first recombinant DNA experiment.

1973   DNA from one organism is combined with plasmid DNA of another organism.

           The scientific community declares a moratorium on further recombinant DNA research.

1975   Cesar Milstein and George Kohler produce monoclonal antibodies by cell fusion (Milstein and Kohler 1975).

1976   The National Institutes of Health issues the first guidelines for genetic engineering, including prohibitions of many types of research.

Table 1.1 Developments in Genetics

Year	Development
1976	The first new corporation devoted to genetic engineering (Genentech) is formed.
1980	The United States Supreme Court rules that existing law permits the patenting of altered microorganisms.
1982	Human insulin, produced by genetically altered microorganisms, is approved for use in the United States and the United Kingdom.
1986	The United States Patent Office approves the patent application for a transgenic mouse.
1989	The United States begins a project to map and sequence the human genome. The first human gene therapy experiments are conducted (for diagnostic rather than therapeutic reasons).

2

What Are We Doing?

Having surveyed the highlights of the scientific and technological revolution in genetics, we step back now to ask interpretive or philosophical questions about ourselves as agents of genetic change. In this way, we are attempting to build a bridge between technology and theology. I will argue that technology and theology are capable of influencing each other. But the connections between them are not at all obvious to most people. Our goal now is to call attention to the bridge between religion and technology.

A central question before us is whether we human beings can even hope to be intentional about our technology. If our relationship with nature is purely unintentional or unconscious and unreflective, if we are in fact incapable of deliberating about long-range goals for our technology, if our relationship with nature is merely that of any other species—namely, a random and purposeless struggle for survival within a changing environment—then of course it is futile to develop a theology of genetic engineering with the hope that this theology will help to guide us. Everything depends on our being able to maintain that conscious, reflective intentionality *at least influences* our biological relationship with nature.

In order to find support for this point, we turn to the world of ancient agriculture and consider how religion and agriculture interacted from the first. In the distant past, we find a world in which religion and biology were not separate spheres, nor were prayer and planting separate acts. While we cannot reintroduce this harmony into our modern era, we can learn from it that our age is not so fragmented, with such clear lines separating religion and science, as we might at first think.

We begin, then, by asking what role human intentionality has in agriculture, both in its origins and in more recent years. From this we turn to a somewhat divergent question that is nonetheless an important interpretive consideration: Do women and men experience nature and technology differently, and should we anticipate that women and men will respond differently to the spread of genetic engineering? Third, we ask how genetic engineering is new when compared with traditional agriculture, especially selective breeding. Finally, we ask about the significance of genetic engineering for the evolution of life on earth. Asking these questions will help us to stand back reflectively from genetic engineering, to understand it within a broader cultural context, and to prepare to consider its theological significance.

Intentionality in Agriculture

Human beings have always altered nature. Even hunter-gatherers have an effect on their environment. While the impact of modern technological society is far greater than that of our ancestors, the important question is not the extent to which we alter nature but whether we do so intentionally, with conscious foresight. If our alterations of nature are not intentional at all, then we cannot argue that we human beings are capable of steering the future of our technological relationship with nature.

Did human beings *intend* to become farmers? According to a cultural explanation of the origins of agriculture, the answer is affirmative. However, according to a more recent co-evolutionary view, the answer is that agriculture is wholly unintentional in origin. The cultural view has enjoyed traditional support, while the co-evolutionary view seeks to account for the origins of agriculture within the framework of current Darwinian theory.

Generally, cultural explanations of agriculture see farming as an intentional human response to the problem of food production. These explanations of agriculture try to show how at least one group of neolithics adopted an agricultural mode of subsistence. Latent within the culture of this group was the capacity to respond consciously to the problem of shortages of food available for hunting and gathering. For example, grains that were gathered may also have been planted intentionally to increase their availability. Once discovered, agricultural techniques spread to other human communities.

Agriculture involves several interrelated techniques: disturbing the soil, planting, weeding or eliminating competitive plants, securing adequate water and nutrients, and harvesting. Of all the agricultural techniques, however, selection or selective breeding is most important. Through selection, domesticated varieties of grain, vegetables, fruits, and farm animals are developed. These domesticates greatly outproduce their wild counterparts in food value. Selection, however, requires centuries in order to achieve significant results. How could the neolithics have intended to become selective breeders, having no prior knowledge that selective breeding works?

An intriguing answer is that religion might have served as a stimulus for agricultural activities, including selective breeding. Intending only to be religious, our neolithic ancestors became agricultural quite by accident. Since we are especially concerned here with the role that religion plays in our biological relationship with nature, this suggestion is particularly interesting.

There is little doubt that religion and agriculture interacted during the pivotal transition period of ten to twelve thousand years ago. The ancient farmer never acted in a merely technological way. Agriculture was inherently and essentially religious from the beginning. That is to say, farming was a religious ritual and act. "To the 'primitive,' agriculture, like all other basic activities, is no merely profane skill. Because it deals with life, and its object is the marvellous growth of that life dwelling in seed, furrow, rain and the spirits of vegetation, it is therefore first and foremost a ritual" (Eliade 1963, p. 331). Agriculture put human beings in direct contact with what were perceived to be divine powers and processes, and the technology of agriculture was a technology for securing the benefits of the gods. Whether the fields were seen as an earth goddess or as the possession of a god, the early farmer would have to be concerned about the response of the divinities to the intrusive acts of clearing and plowing the land. The rain came from a sky god or a storm god whose cooperation was necessary for agricultural success. Knowing how to secure that cooperation was a part of religio-agricultural technique.

But did religion cause agriculture to occur? How could religious practices and beliefs prompt our neolithic ancestors to take up agriculture? Various causal links between religion and agriculture have been suggested (cf. Rindos 1984, p. 11). It has been proposed, for example, that keeping animals for religious sacrifices led to the domestication of herds of cattle (Heiser 1973, p. 27). Animals such as wild cattle, goats, and sheep, it is argued, were sacrificed for cultic reasons before they were domesticated. If so, then it is imaginable that our ancestors captured these wild animals, brought them to the place of sacrifice, and kept them alive until the right time for the sacrifice. This practice may have led to the keeping of a small herd for just such a purpose, and eventually to the breeding and perpetuation of the herd (Heiser 1973, p. 27). The agricultural use of these animals for milk, meat, and other products would then have followed.

It has been suggested, too, that the rite of burial included the burying of seeds gathered from food plants (Heiser 1973, pp. 28–29). Unwittingly, primitive human beings were thereby planting seeds in soil that was turned and fertilized. Amazed by the productivity of these grains, they may have continued to dig, plant seeds, and accompany the planting with a ritual sacrifice—either human or of a domesticated animal—thinking that it was the religious act of sacrifice rather than the organic matter that caused the productivity. The widespread linkage between planting and sacrifice gives this highly speculative idea some plausibility.

The religious explanation of agriculture has an advantage over other cultural explanations, especially in accounting for the process of selective breeding. The great problem faced by general cultural explanations is accounting for the foresight and intentionality that would have been required among the first farmers who engaged in selective breeding. Selective breeding is a slow and unpredictable process. If one did not know in advance that it would eventually produce a better crop, one's initial results would not lead to this observation. How could the first agriculturalists have been motivated to continue to select the best seeds for replanting? How could the first farmers have foreseen the advantages of domesticates over wild grains? And how could they have intentionally set out on a course of action, the long-range benefit of which they could not have foreseen? "Are we to attribute a precognizance to Neolithic people that we would deny ourselves?" (Rindos 1984, p. 3).

The religious explanation offers a relatively simple account of how the first farmers were motivated to select, save, and plant the best of the grains and of other domesticated plants and animals. Making an offering to the gods by scattering the best seeds was not intended to produce a better crop, just to please the gods. Since the gods were evidently pleased, the practice continued, and over many years the crop improved as an unintended by-product of a religious act. But why not give the gods just any seeds?

> We might ask why would man save his best seeds for planting rather than eating them? Obviously, if the seeds were for the gods, they would have been the largest, most nearly perfect, or perhaps from plants showing unusual characteristics. We might postulate that artificial selection began to operate with the first offering of seeds to the spirits of the plants. (Heiser 1973, p. 31)

The harvests became ever more productive, and the gods appeared to reward this technique of worship. According to this explanation, selective breeding began as a religious offering.

Rindos (1984) rejects all cultural explanations of agriculture, religious ones among them. However, he recognizes the simplicity and plausibility of religious explanations over other cultural explanations. "I must confess a certain weakness for these religious theories of the origin of agriculture. . . . They. . . have the advantage of explaining directly, and in one simple step, the invention of agricultural techniques such as planting or the saving of the best seed" (Rindos 1984, p. 11).

Rindos continues by pointing out a potential problem that arises when we consider religion to be the explanation of agriculture: "Religious theories must be rejected when confronted by the evidence that agricultural systems have been developed by other animals (unless we are willing to attribute religion to ants or termites)" (1984, p. 11). In this comment, however, Rindos seems to ignore the fact that insect agricultural behavior is acquired and transmitted through genetic or biological evolution, while human agriculture is acquired and transmitted through *cultural* evolution. Human beings do not carry genes for agricultural behavior. We are genetically the same, for all practical purposes, as our hunter-gatherer forebears. Termites and ants have complex social systems, but these are acquired and transmitted through *genetic* evolution. Our capacity for society may have its foundation in our genes, but the wide variety and changing forms of human social order show that human social order is cultural.

In spite of the attraction of religious explanations of the origins of agriculture, they do have a serious flaw. Religion apparently predates agriculture by thousands of years. If religion caused the rise of agriculture, why did it not do so sooner? What development occurred in religion itself to prompt it to become a form of religion favorable to agriculture? The answer must be the obvious one: Religion that arises in an agricultural community favors agriculture, while religion in preagricultural societies does not. Religion does not explain the origins of agriculture, but agriculture itself explains the origin of forms of religion that encourage agriculture.

If the origin of agriculture is not explained by religion or culture, what does explain it? Rindos proposes a co-evolutionary model derived from Darwinian theory and, indeed, from suggestions made by Darwin himself. Darwin discusses artificial selection or selection of traits by human beings as an analogy for natural selection, which he postulates as that natural process which gives organic evolution the appearance of purpose and directionality. In his discussion of artificial selection, Darwin distinguishes between unconscious and conscious (or methodical) selection (Darwin 1968 [1859]). Rindos develops Darwin's suggestion about unconscious selection into a theory of the origin of agriculture.

By gathering seeds, damaging other plants, dropping the seeds accidentally, and countless other inadvertencies, human beings were related extensively to the development of certain species of plants. Such a biological relationship between two species changes inevitably, occasionally in a mutually beneficial way. Individuals of one species select traits from among the individuals of the second species that are beneficial to the first species. For example, larger grains are beneficial to human beings and are therefore selected by being scattered more widely than other grains. Through this selection process, those individual grains that are selected are dispersed more widely and therefore reproduce more frequently than those that are not selected, thereby altering the distribution of desirable traits in the next generation. To be part of a co-evolutionary process, however, means that both species select individuals of the other species (thereby increasing the reproductive chances of those that are selected) and benefit from doing so. Human beings benefit from a wider distribution of larger grains, while the grains benefit from a larger population of increasingly dependent human beings who distribute their seeds.

Through this symbiotic interaction, both species in the relationship evolve. The human evolution occurs primarily as cultural evolution,

while the genetic structure of the plants evolves. The edible plants benefited greatly by allowing themselves to be eaten, thereby inducing
human beings to distribute and protect them. Human beings benefited
by serving or cultivating the plants.

Human beings did not intend to domesticate the plants any more
than the plants intended to domesticate human beings. Neither *foresaw*
the effect of changes in their relationship.

> If domesticated plants arose by means of an interactive process between
> humans and plants, it is absurd to speak of either intent or adaptation. We
> might equally well describe the evolution of domesticated plants by
> saying that the plants chose humans to protect and disseminate them, or
> that the plants adapted by using humans to increase their own fitness. . . .
> Plants have contributed as much to the evolution of the agroecology as
> have humans, for it was plants that created the situation in which certain
> types of human behaviors became selectively advantageous. (Rindos 1984,
> pp. 93, 142)

We might say that certain agricultural plants have "domesticated"
human beings, for they selected those human behaviors most advanta-
geous to them. While the human population has multiplied dramatically
since the advent of agriculture, we have not kept pace with the reproductive success of agricultural plants such as wheat.

By interacting with plants and by *unintentionally modifying* that interaction, human beings have evolved (culturally) with plants within a
complex, symbiotic relationship. The advantage of the co-evolutionary
explanation of the origins of agriculture is that it does not require that we
assume early human beings intended to domesticate crops and animals.

While human intent does not cause agriculture to begin, human beings
have engaged in conscious reflection on agriculture.

> To deny intentionality, of course, is not to deny consciousness, [and] I am
> not claiming that people are incapable of reflection but only that reflection
> and consciousness are incapable of causing the initiation of cultural
> changes such as agriculture. . . . It is obvious that at some point agricul-
> tural humans became aware of being involved in a mode of subsistence
> that differed from that of other cultures, or from that which might be
> imagined as possible. (Rindos 1984, pp. 98–99)

Rindos goes on to say, however, that "consciousness is reflective, not
predictive" (Rindos 1984, p. 99).

Ironically, however, Rindos concludes his highly competent study, in
which he attempts to prove the irrelevance of intentionality as an explanation for agriculture, with an invocation to intentionality to save us
from future disaster:

> The spread of agriculture resembles the spread of a pathology such as

rabies in that the symptoms facilitate the dissemination of the disease; I would hope that an awareness of the processes by which agriculture developed may act as a spur to us to gather the information that may permit us to become as successfully intentional as we have so glibly claimed to be. (Rindos 1984, p. 285)

But if intentionality did not contribute at all to the directing of previous human behavior, it is hard to see how one can have any confidence that intentionally will direct our future behavior.

While the co-evolutionary view of the origins of agriculture is persuasive, there is no reason to draw reductionist conclusions from it and to portray human consciousness and intentionality as merely responsive. Unlike termite agriculture, human agricultural behavior is *cultural*, not genetic. As a set of cultural rites, agriculture cannot help but interact with all other elements of our culture, including religion. Human consciousness may be a response to agriculture rather than the cause of it. But once this consciousness is generated, it exerts its own generative pressure upon the future development of agriculture.

Human consciousness, which is communicated through culture and religion, does far more than merely respond to our biological relationship with nature. Consciousness generates outcomes in biology that cannot be explained if culture is ignored. Consciousness does reflect on what is, but out of that reflection it envisions what might be. In religious and moral categories, it envisions what should be and motivates individuals and communities to struggle for that which is identified as good. Religious and moral ideas reflect on the present and guide us in the unfolding of the future.

To see more clearly how culture and religion have biological consequences, let us return for a moment to Darwin's distinction between unconscious and conscious selection. Darwin saw that human selection, for the most part, is unconscious or unintentional. Rindos's theory of agriculture uses Darwin's unconscious selection but largely ignores the significance of conscious selection. For millennia, however, the human act of selection has been a consciously informed act. Conscious selection is the process by which human beings, informed by cultural considerations, act intentionally on the genetic inheritance of other organisms. The traits desired consciously by the breeder become predictive of the result that is achieved through breeding. In Darwin's view, *consciousness is predictive and therefore generative*. Breeders envision the traits they desire in a plant or animal species and set out intentionally to breed a specimen with just those traits.

I will quote Darwin at length concerning the high level of skill with which the breeders of his era created what they intended to create:

Breeders habitually speak of an animal's organisation as something quite plastic, which they can model almost as they please. If I had space I could quote numerous passages to this effect from highly competent authorities. Youatt, who was probably better acquainted with the works of agricultur- alists than almost any other individual, and who was himself a very good judge of an animal, speaks of the principle of selection as "that which enables the agriculturalist, not only to modify the character of his flock, but to change it altogether. It is the magician's wand, by means of which he may summon into life whatever form and mould he pleases." Lord Somerville, speaking of what breeders have done for sheep, says, —"It would seem as if they had chalked out upon a wall a form perfect in itself, and then had given it existence." That most skillful breeder, Sir John Sebright, used to say, with respect to pigeons, that "he would produce any given feather in three years, but it would take him six years to obtain head and beak." (Darwin 1968 [1859], p. 90)

Human beings did not intend to become farmers. But once agricul- tural behaviors were adopted, human beings thought about what they were doing and wondered how they could do it more successfully. Human beings became farmers, not merely unintentional distributors of seeds. Once conscious intentionality emerges, it inevitably exerts some influence upon how human beings determine that certain traits are desirable and others objectionable. Culture, including religion, sharpens our goals by distinguishing the desirable from the objectionable. Reli- gion in particular identifies the benefits that we intend to achieve through agriculture. Through religion, we communicate our desires, addressing them as petitions to the divine and thereby committing ourselves and our co-workers to their accomplishment.

We human beings are capable of breeding desired characteristics into plants and animals. We are highly successful at making agriculture more productive. We have turned these intentions into results. But even as we have succeeded in achieving these intended goals, we have reaped unin- tended consequences. Our agriculture has damaged the land, poisoned the water, and narrowed the genetic diversity of the plants and animals upon which we have allowed ourselves to become almost totally dependent.

These are the frightening ironies of agriculture: The more we succeed in our intention of making agriculture productive and efficient, the more we cause unintentional damage to the environment. When we begin to deliberately alter the land for agriculture, our impact on the land becomes more destructive. When we consciously engage in selective breeding, we dramatically narrow the gene pool of valuable plants and animals. The most primitive forms of agriculture (that is, the least intentional) were also the least destructive. They were the least disruptive of the environ- ment and had the least impact on other species. The more we intend to be farmers, the greater our impact on nature, for as human intentionality increases, so does the unintended damage to the environment.

Beyond his effects on his own species, man has exterminated many others.

Still others he has modified by artificial selection and by inducing, or at least preserving, mutant forms. Man has brutally and dangerously modified environments, both his own and those of other species. Man's cultural evolution has had enormous repercussions for the biological evolution of all organisms; it seems unlikely that any species has escaped unscathed. (Dobzhansky and Boesiger 1983, p. 101)

As we become more successful in achieving our immediate, short-range goal of increased productivity, the long-term consequences of our actions multiply. "Many of our best efforts at increasing agricultural productivity should be expected to increase the vulnerability of the system; the best efforts of our ancestors to improve the productivity of their systems had a similar effect" (Rindos 1984, p. 285). Unintentionally we have altered other species, transformed the global environment, and increased our own numbers exponentially.

Our effect upon the land has been pervasive. Land that was once forested, and in which our hunter-gatherer ancestors lived without serious ecological impact, has been cleared for agriculture. After years and years of cultivation, however, land loses its fertility, and next it becomes useful as pastureland. This widespread pattern of transition from forest to field to pasture has meant serious environmental degradation. In the temperate regions of Europe and North America, the environmental effect has not been as pronounced as in the Near East and the tropics. Land that once was forested—having been cleared, farmed, and grazed—has been left arid and barren. "Land, once left open, does not revert to forest or, if it was steppe to begin with, it merely remains the desert it has become. . . . Agriculture takes more organic matter out of the soil than it puts back" (Zeuner 1963, pp. 31–32). Recent use of fertilizer and pesticides, together with tilling practices that permit widespread erosion, has accelerated the damage. The total global environmental effect of the human practice of agriculture over the past ten thousand years has been devastating.

Modern selective breeding is another cause for concern. "Modern plant-breeding is a very special type of domestication—in essence it is an attempt to be intentional about domesticate evolution. How effective this attempt ultimately proves to be is an issue with potentially grave consequences" (Rindos 1984, p. 164). Dobzhansky and Boesiger (1983) comment, "Many modern agricultural specialists are gravely concerned over the loss of genetic diversity that resides for the moment among the many breeds and varieties of animals and plants that have been developed through centuries and millennia of diversifying artificial selection" (Dobzhansky and Boesiger 1983, p. 3). We have also reduced the number of plant species upon which we depend for food to the point where today, we human beings receive most of our food from twenty species (National Academy of Sciences 1975).

Concl *1*

The more we improve any component of the agricultural system, the more the system as a whole becomes vulnerable. Modern agriculture is dangerously unstable. Environmental degradation and the narrowing of the genetic base of agricultural plants and animals have brought us to a precarious point. We have succeeded in our intent to make agriculture productive and efficient, but in doing so we have also made it risky in evolutionary terms.

Concl— Our point here is not so much the extent of our damage as the fact that it is almost entirely unintended. No one intended to reduce forest to pasture, and no one saw it coming. "Primitive man, and indeed civilized man until quite recently, was unaware of this, hence vast regions have changed their aspect completely, and always to quasi-drier conditions, since the beginnings of the Neolithic" (Zeuner 1963, p. 33). Changes of climate or habitat usually occur too slowly for any individual to observe, and so most human beings make the mistake of believing that their natural environment is largely unchanging. Because of the combined impact of the industrial revolution and modern agriculture in recent centuries, some environmental changes have occurred so rapidly that we cannot help but notice them. These transformations of nature have been both unintentional and, until recently, unforeseen. After all, we only intended to produce better harvests.

To be intentional is to stand back from what we are doing and to ask what we want to achieve, and then to set out with our goal in mind. Intentionality, however, can be more or less long-range in its vision. For example, our intention can be to get something to eat, to secure a harvest next season, or to secure a food supply for our descendants a thousand years hence. Mid-level intentionality, focusing on next year's harvest, is proving to be dangerous, for it pits the goals of the foreseeable future against the needs of a more distant future.

We have greatly outproduced our hunter-gatherer ancestors, both in our food supply and in our damage to biological systems. Dependent as we are upon the quantity of food we now produce, we can hardly return to a hunter-gatherer relationship with nature. We cannot become unintentional about feeding ourselves, hoping that a return to the lifestyle of Adam and Eve will restore nature to Eden.

What we can do is to aim at a new consciousness, a new intentionality about our role on earth. We can aim at more than large harvests and the productiveness of new varieties of plants and animals. We can also aim intentionally at the sustainability of our biological niche in nature and at biodiversity. Through this new and higher intentionality, we may yet learn to modify our own short-term goals, demanding that our desire for a productive agriculture be reconciled to the sustainability of our place on earth.

The emergence of genetic engineering, in combination with other technologies, may provide potential solutions to some of the problems we have created through agriculture. For instance, genetic engineering offers hope for an agriculture less dependent upon chemical fertilizers and pesticides. However, if genetic engineering merely serves our limited intention for efficient and effective agriculture, we should expect the dangerous and unintended by-products of our actions to continue, probably at an accelerated pace. On the other hand, if genetic engineering is accompanied by a religious and cultural transformation and by the attainment of a higher intentionality that ascribes worth to environmental stability and biodiversity, then genetic engineering may help us undo some of the unintended damage of agriculture.

Male and Female in Biology and Culture

Will genetic engineering affect women and men differently? Should we anticipate that women will typically respond to some aspects of genetic engineering differently from the way men will typically respond? These are intriguing questions with significant public policy implications. There is already good reason, given the popularity of feminist critiques of reproductive technologies (such as the film *The Handmaid's Tale*) to think that men and women will see genetic engineering in quite different lights. In order to understand some of the reasons for this difference, it is useful to consider how women and men were affected differently by agriculture.

Since hunter-gatherer societies generally relied upon the gathering abilities of the females and the hunting abilities of the males, agriculture probably developed from the women's gathering wild grains, and so it may have been originally pursued largely by women. This change in the source of human livelihood undoubtedly took millennia to complete. During the long transition, men may have continued to hunt while women planted and gathered crops. Eliade (1978) attributes early agriculture largely to women: "Since women played a decisive part in the domestication of plants, they became the owners of the cultivated fields, which raises their social position and creates characteristic institutions, such as, for example, matrilocation, the husband being obliged to live in his wife's house" (Eliade 1978, p. 40). The transition to early agriculture may have meant social ascendancy for women.

Other scholars suggest a more complex pattern, summarized by Ester Boserup (1970) in the following generalizations, drawn from the variations in modern agriculture:

> In very sparsely populated regions where shifting cultivation is used, men do little farm work, the women doing most. In somewhat more densely populated regions, where the agricultural system is that of extensive plough cultivation, women do little farm work and men do much more. Finally, in regions of intensive cultivation of irrigated land, both men and

women must put hard work into agriculture in order to earn enough to support a family on a small piece of land. (Boserup 1970, p. 35)

If this is true, then it is likely that women were predominant in early agriculture, and that men became more predominant with the use of the plow. This corresponds to the general cultural and religious responses to agriculture in the earliest periods and until the use of the plow. In the earliest settings, the reproductive capacities of women were held in awe, especially since the fertility of the fields and flocks was seen as depending upon the fertility of the women. This sense of awe and of communal dependence probably undergirded whatever social ascendancy women may have enjoyed during this period. Women were not only predominant among the first practitioners of agriculture: They incarnated and enhanced its mystical powers in their own fertility. "One of the salient features in all agricultural societies is the solidarity they see between the fertility of the land and that of their women" (Eliade 1963, p. 256). Typically, early agricultural communities thought of the earth as a fertile goddess to be honored and respected. Thus fertility, divinity, and femaleness formed an essential unity upon which life depended. As grains were gathered and unintentionally sown, it was thought that the earth goddess brought forth of herself, through a process of parthenogenesis. No male action was needed. The female was fertility itself. In the earliest phases of agriculture, men tended to remain in the role of the hunter while women gathered grains and began to plant.

As agriculture developed, villages became larger and game became more scarce, and men turned to farming (including herding). Agriculture itself was also transformed into a more active process by which the earth goddess was increasingly exploited for human benefit. The development of the plow is most crucial in this transition. In many early agricultural societies, the plow was seen as a phallus that fertilized a passive, plowed female earth. "To identify woman with a furrow implies an identification of phallus with spade, of tilling with the act of generation" (Eliade 1963, p. 259). No longer was the earth goddess capable of producing by herself. Indeed, she is no longer even thought of as the *earth* goddess but as a goddess of agriculture whose fertility depends upon the activity of a fertilizing god. Heterosexual reproduction replaced female parthenogenesis. The female earth required a plow, and in this transition she became increasingly passive. Fertility was brought to her. We can imagine the effects of this agri-religious transformation upon the social status of women.

Contemporary feminist writers emphasize that our reproductive technology is embedded in a social context that is ancient in origin and typically patriarchal in form. Often, the connection between agricultural use of animals and the medical treatment of women is made. For example, in the opening chapter of *The Mother Machine*, Gena Corea moves from an account of the first human artificial insemination to a description of a similar procedure on a cattle farm (Corea 1985, pp. 1213). She refers to the ancient goddess-centered religion, claiming that the decline of this era occurred as men gained control of reproduction (Corea 1985, pp. 60–62). Genetic engineering extends this male control of reproduction, Corea argues. In vitro fertilization leaves the newly fertilized egg accessible to technical alteration. "Once pharmacrats develop techniques for genetic engineering, they could adjust the embryo's genetic makeup before transferring that embryo" to the mother (Corea 1985, p. 133).

What characterizes a feminist perspective, according to Christine Overall, is not the rejection of technology but the insistence that it be viewed from the perspective of women. Reproductive technologies "will affect human lives—but, in particular, they will affect *women's* lives, and that potential does not always receive the emphasis it deserves" (Overall 1987, p. 1). On the question of whether genetic techniques should be used for sex selection of children, Overall is highly cautious about misuse but is not categorically opposed.

> There are some individual cases—perhaps, in practice, rare—in which there are good (although perhaps not sufficient) reasons for the use of sex preselection techniques: that is, those in which the prospective parents seek to avoid the risk for their offspring of sex-linked diseases and those in which they choose the sex of the child on the basis of a desire for what I have called sexual similarity or complementarity. Hence the use of technologies for fetal sex preselection is not necessarily sexist—although it may very well be, and given present sex preferences, the dangers of their use are considerable. (Overall 1987, pp. 34–35)

Overall notes that not all feminist writers are equally critical of reproductive technologies, although she believes that the tendency toward criticism will increase: "More recent feminist writers . . . have witnessed the implementation of the 'technological fix' in reproduction and have been less enthusiastic about the potential benefits of reproductive technology. . . . Feminists have foreseen several possible reproductive futures, both bad and good" (Overall 1987, pp. 10, 210).

The feminist insistence that technology's effect on women be considered seriously is unarguable, as is the claim that these technologies have a social history that shape their design and use. In the distant past, religion symbolized the reproductive differences between male and female. Gods and goddesses portrayed symbols of ultimacy and power, while priestesses and priests wielded the technology of social control. Our age is not entirely different, for we still struggle over the gender of God and clergy, intuitively recognizing that the underlying issue has to do with the social power. If Christianity is able to reform itself in light of its own feminist critique, it may be in a position to encourage a broader social awareness of the concerns feminists are raising about reproductive technologies.

The Novelty of Genetic Engineering

In what ways is genetic engineering a new mode of human relationship with nature? A great deal depends upon how we answer this question, for the more novelty we see in genetic engineering, the more we are likely to fear it. Indeed, one tactic of critics of genetic engineering is to emphasize its novelty. For example, some critics use titles such as *Who Should Play God?* for books discussing the ethical implications of genetic engineering (Howard and Rifkin 1977). Another critic, Robert Sinsheimer, comments, "Genetic engineering is a whole new technology. To view it as merely another technological development may make sense for those who invest in its commercial exploitation. But such a view is myopic for anyone concerned with the future of humanity" (Sinsheimer 1983, p. 14).

I do not want to indulge in such overstatements of the novelty of genetic engineering. There are, however, at least four important ways in which genetic engineering signifies a new human relationship with the biological. These four ways have to do with human intentionality, speed, the way in which genetic engineering acts directly upon DNA, and the explosion of biological knowledge triggered by developments in molecular genetics. While they are less dramatic than the rhetoric of "playing God," these are serious innovations in the history of evolution. Let us consider them more fully.

Human Intentionality

The chemical processes of genetic engineering are nothing new. They have all occurred in nature, almost since life began. Restriction enzymes, ligases, plasmids, and viruses are all natural agents. They are constantly cutting and splicing the DNA of all organisms, including that in our own bodies. Without their continuous activity, biological evolution would have much less genetic variety on which to draw. Speaking of the evolutionary significance of some of these processes now used in genetic engineering, Bernard Davis comments, "Their evolutionary significance is profound. For while genetic variety arises ultimately from mutations, it would develop very slowly if mutations could accumulate only within a direct line of descent" (Davis 1980, p. 79). Far from being new, these chemical processes are as old as life. We owe our evolution to them. We might term these natural process "natural recombination."

Nevertheless, the *technology* of genetic engineering is strikingly new. While the chemical processes of natural recombination are billions of years old, and while they occur naturally all around us and even inside us, *as technology*—conscious, intentional, and purposive—genetic engineering or artificial recombination is new. When human beings first understood the biochemical processes of natural recombination and used these processes for human objectives, something new emerged. For the first time, these processes came under the conscious direction not just of human beings but of any species. Our species, capable of consciousness, now uses these biochemical processes to attain specific, intentional ends. The intentional action of a particular species has entered the microbiological level.

Through genetic engineering, human values are expressed at the microbiological level. Once we learn how to use the processes of genetic alteration, we make choices whether to use them, and toward what objectives. When we discover a new technique, we face choices as to its use and the limits of that use. We patent it, license it, and set a price on it, further defining its value and limits. More important, we imagine still more information and techniques we would like to have, and we set about in research to discover them. All of these actions are grounded in human values, but through genetic engineering, they have an impact on microbiological processes.

Through agriculture, human choice entered the biological realm at the level of selection and altered the evolutionary processes of many plants and animals. For the most part, this was an unconscious process: Human beings acted without foresight or long-range planning. In recent centuries, however, plant and animal breeders have been able to achieve very specific, desired goals. Human moral choice acted on evolution by *altering the processes of selection*.

In addition, human beings have changed environments, contributing further to the alteration of the selection process. Evolution proceeds because the environment selects those individuals that are relatively more fit. When the environment changes, its selection criteria will change. Human beings have changed the environment, usually unintentionally but also as the result of conscious choice. Consequently, human choice has acted upon the evolutionary process by *environmental alteration*.

Now, with genetic engineering, human choice has entered the biological process at a *third* point, namely that of *mutation at the microbiological level*. Until genetic engineering, the microbiological level lay beyond the direct reach of conscious choice. Breeders were limited to those genes already present in the gene pool of the breeding population. Now, to the small extent that genetic engineering has occurred, our choices have skewed the value-neutrality of the microbiological in the direction of our values and desires. No longer is the microbiological level value-free: We human beings have entered it and left the imprint of our choices.

The Speed of Change

When compared to classic techniques of selective breeding, genetic engineering is fast. Through the use of classic techniques, breeders of plants and animals can produce nearly any desired trait, given enough time. Genetic engineering, potentially, cuts this time to a mere fraction.

This has two implications that are qualitative in significance. First, some lines of work that are not economical or practical using classic methods now become feasible. While this does not mean that we can do things we could not do before, it certainly does mean that now we will try to do things we would not have bothered to try before. In this respect, genetic engineering is significantly new.

The other implication is that with increased speed, there is less time for human beings individually or collectively to reflect on the effects of their work. Where classic animal breeders took many generations of animals to develop a certain trait and therefore had ample time for themselves and their neighbors to reflect on the true desirability of their work, genetic engineering takes place quickly. Often the public finds out after the work is finished, especially if proprietary secrets are at stake. Speed of development, therefore, means less time to reflect, and this enhances the likelihood of serious miscalculation of the true desirability of the line of research and often effectively eliminates public participation in that reflection.

The Effect of Genetic Engineering on DNA

Genetic engineering makes it possible for human beings to act directly upon DNA. Selective breeding acts by selecting *traits* and thereby indirectly affects the genetic material. Genetic engineering acts directly upon the genetic material itself. Some have felt that scientists are now intruding upon an inner sanctuary of life, a sacred mystery of genetic givenness that should only be received (from God or from nature) with gratitude, never manipulated or engineered. The model of the DNA molecule itself, with its intricate spiral structure, its vast amounts of information, and above all its unique ability to replicate itself, enhances this sense of mystery and sacredness in the popular imagination. Now, some fear, scientists are cutting, rearranging, and mapping this mystery.

Is this the violation of a sacred precinct, an act of human arrogance toward nature? Robert Sinsheimer, for example, asks, "What happens to the reverence for life when life is our creation, our plaything?" (Sinsheimer 1983, p. 14). DNA comes to symbolize life itself, and genetic engineering represents life's manipulation and desecration. "For thousands of years human beings have been fusing, melting, soldering, forging, and burning inanimate matter into economic utilities. Now they are about to begin the process of slicing, recombining, inserting, and stitching living material into economic realities" (Rifkin 1983, p. 11). For Rifkin, this is a dangerous and arrogant act, reducing life (i.e., DNA) to another raw material for engineers and industrialists. Underlying both Sinsheimer's and Rifkin's protest is the conviction that DNA is more than matter—it is life, and therefore it is sacred.

In fairness to Sinsheimer and Rifkin, we recall the definition of genetic engineering that we borrowed from the report of the President's

Commission (1982), namely, that genetic engineering is "the directed manipulation of the genetic material itself" (p. 92). Sinsheimer and Rifkin, however, make a philosophical, even theological, leap when they speak of genetic material as life. Life, for them, is a distinctive metaphysical category, off limits to technical manipulation. Rifkin laments, "All living things are drained of their aliveness and turned into abstract messages. Life becomes a code to be deciphered. There is no longer any question of sacredness or inviolability" (Rifkin 1983, p. 228). The report of the President's Commission (1982) notes a similar concern: "By identifying DNA and learning how to manipulate it, science seems to have reduced people to a set of malleable molecules that can be interchanged with those of species that people regard as inferior" (p. 54). The report continues by rejecting this fear as not well considered.

Is DNA the essence of life? Is it any more arrogant or sacrilegious to cut DNA than to cut living tissue, as in surgery? It is hard to imagine a scientific or philosophical argument that would successfully support the metaphysical or moral uniqueness of DNA. Even DNA's capacity to replicate does not elevate this molecule to a higher metaphysical or moral level. Replication and sexual reproduction are important capacities, crucial in biology. But they are hardly the stuff of sanctity.

Once, metal was thought to be sacred. In widely scattered ancient cultures there was a shared conviction of "the sacredness of metal and consequently the ambivalent, eccentric and mysterious character of all mining and metallurgical operations" (Eliade 1962, pp. 99–100). If for some philosophic or religious reason we believed that DNA is more sacred than any other complex chemical, then it would follow that we should be very cautious about acting directly upon it. But such a conviction of DNA's sanctity is not grounded in Western philosophic or religious traditions. Employing it now, in the context of genetic engineering, is arbitrary. To think of genetic material as the exclusive realm of divine grace and creativity is to reduce God to the level of restriction enzymes, viruses, and sexual reproduction. Treating DNA as matter—complicated, awe-inspiring, and elaborately coded, but matter nonetheless—is not in itself sacrilegious.

The Knowledge Explosion in Biology

Because it provides powerful new techniques for biological research, genetic engineering is being accompanied by an explosion of knowledge in biology. On the whole, this knowledge will be beneficial in helping the human species understand and care for the biosphere. Since we are biological organisms, the knowledge that we will acquire will also be knowledge about ourselves.

As individuals, many of us in the future will have more knowledge—and a different kind of knowledge—about ourselves than our ancestors ever had. Increasingly, we and our potential offspring will be screened genetically. As adults, we will be screened for genetic defects we might pass on to our children or for genetic conditions that might leave us more vulnerable to certain environmental conditions (hazardous chemicals in the workplace, for example). Our unborn offspring will be increasingly screened and judged for their genetic viability. What parents do with genetically defective fetuses will, of course, be a new and agonizing dilemma. How people will respond to the knowledge that they carry recessive genes for a number of serious (perhaps lethal) genetic disorders remains to be seen.

More important, genetic engineering and related analytic techniques are providing new knowledge of the human species. Ready or not, we are beginning to learn more about our evolution, our behavior, and our genetic diversity than we have ever known before. Given our historic social sensitivity to this knowledge, we can see its coming as a mixed blessing.

New approaches to human evolution using molecular biology are yielding striking new conjectures about our evolutionary history and our proximity to other species. Analysis of mitochondrial DNA (which has a strictly maternal line of descent) suggests that all human beings may have descended from a common mother, appropriately referred to as "Eve," living in central Africa some 200,000 years ago (Cann, Stoneking, and Wilson 1987). Using similar techniques to analyze the Y chromosome, which only males have, a group of researchers conjectured that there may have been a first human father, Adam, who also lived in Africa 200,000 years ago and resembled present-day pygmies (Gibbons 1991a, pp. 378–80). While these preliminary results are highly tentative, they indicate the kind of uses to which molecular biology will be put in the future (Gibbons 1991b, pp. 872–74).

In this regard, the mapping of the human genome will be highly significant. Not only will this research yield helpful information about diseases that are caused by a single genetic defect, but other patterns will no doubt emerge, suggesting multigenetic bases for more complex human traits, including mental illnesses and perhaps personality traits such as extroversion and neuroticism. How we distinguish the genetically normal from the defective will be a difficult question. Furthermore, the combination of genetics research techniques with statistical studies may yield results that touch off a new round in the classic debate over the influence of genetic heredity versus environment.

This debate over heredity versus environment is exacerbated by broad societal concerns over race and ethnicity. Some studies claim that genetic differences between racial and ethnic groups are less wide than differences within each identifiable group (Zuckerman 1990, pp. 1297–1303). But as a greater knowledge of human genetics develops, the study of the genetics of race will inevitably be undertaken, amidst inevitable controversy. Studies of ethnic variations in Europe have already been made. One study of the peoples of the Iberian Peninsula has produced a kind of ethnic or genetic map, claiming that the Basques are the least genetically related to agricultural infiltrators who entered Europe thousands of years ago from the Middle East (Bertranpetit and Cavalli-Sforza 1991). This thesis is supported by genetic samples drawn from across the continent of Europe (Sokal, Oden, and Wilson 1991). Some researchers are urging that genetic samples be gathered quickly from vanishing indigenous populations worldwide (Roberts 1991). Inevitably, similar studies will explore the origins of and the differences between other racial and ethnic groups. These reports are being made at a time when ethnic consciousness is increasing.

Genetic engineering is giving us new knowledge about all of nature, about ourselves as a species interdependent upon and closely related to other species, and about each of us as individuals. This new knowledge is laden with social and moral meaning. In the case of genetic screening, federal guidelines require that screening centers interpret the genetic information. But there is no comparable requirement, nor can there be, that the new genetic understanding of the human species be interpreted in a kind of species-wide genetic counseling. Who will interpret to us, the human race, what we are about to learn about ourselves? Who will be expected to say what this new knowledge, wonderful as it is, means for our lives, our origins, our human dilemma, and our destiny? No answers to these questions will be found in scientific research. They will arise only as this research is interpreted within a broader cultural and religious framework.

Evolution and Genetic Engineering

Speaking of the discovery of recombinant DNA techniques, Nicholas Wade opens *The Ultimate Experiment: Man-Made Evolution* with this comment: "A turning point has been reached in the study of life. A turning point of such consequence that it may make its mark not just in the history of science but perhaps even in the evolution of life itself" (Wade 1977, p. 1). The book concludes with this sentence: "Hitherto evolution has seemed as inexorable and irreversible a process as time or entropy; now at least there lies almost within man's grasp a tool for manipulating the force that shaped him, for controlling his own creator" (Wade 1977, p. 155).

Will genetic engineering have an impact on the course of evolution? Undoubtedly it will. Virtually everything we do has an impact on evolution. But the impact of genetic engineering on the course of evolution is easily overstated. This impact may turn out to be less than our impact through artificial selection. In agriculture, for instance, the greatest impact of genetic engineering might be as an enhancement of artificial selection. In the previous chapter, we noted that in the application of genetic engineering to agricultural animals, the most significant use of genetic techniques might come through screening of desirable traits prior to implantation of embryos (Womack 1987, p. 68). If this is true, then ironically the greatest contribution of genetic technology (in this field of application) would be through the enhancement of artificial selection, not through artificial recombination.

Nevertheless, some have argued that genetic engineering poses a threat to the evolutionary process, potentially altering its course in unforeseeable and dangerous ways (Chargaff 1976; Sinsheimer 1975, 1983). They warn that we are quickly taking evolution into our own hands, defying the wisdom of hundreds of millions of years with our own short-term objectives. They fear that by creating novel genetic combinations, we will release organisms that can exploit the environment in unpredictable ways, perhaps making it uninhabitable for ourselves. To support the argument, they cite the dramatic impact of the introduction of rabbits to Australia or kudzu to the southeastern United States.

These fears are not unfounded. The question of environmental release of altered organisms should remain a major concern. But the impact of genetic engineering on the course of evolution is easily overdrawn. We have already affected the process of natural selection, thereby altering the path of evolution. But our impact on selection has been absorbed into a dynamic, co-evolutionary process: Our selective pressure on a particular species has been the occasion for that species' evolution, which has in turn affected our own (largely cultural) evolution. What this means is that while we have had a considerable impact on evolution, we have not stood back, as if we ourselves were somehow immune to the processes, and consciously steered its course from a safe, reflective distance. Rather, through intentional and unintentional acts, we have embedded ourselves within co-evolutionary processes with many other species. We could not have done otherwise.

With genetic engineering, we now have the capacity to affect the evolutionary process at the point of mutation and recombination. If our past activity of artificial selection is any reliable guide to the future impact of genetic engineering, we may predict that genetic engineering will best be seen as a co-evolutionary relationship between our species and many others. It is tempting to say that through genetic engineering, we are taking evolution into our own hands. The truth is less dramatic. Through genetic engineering, we are entering a new phase of a co-evolutionary relationship with other species. Far from taking evolution into our own hands, we are being taken into the hands of a dynamic process over which we will have little overarching control. This observation is not made as an argument against genetic engineering, any more than it would be an argument against agriculture. It is merely an attempt to describe modestly and accurately the era of evolutionary history we are entering. If the critics of genetic engineering prefer that evolution be left outside human control, they may be reassured: Genetic engineering will not change this fundamental truth. The co-evolutionary process will remain bigger than we are. Within it, our technology and culture will evolve, even as we contribute to the evolution of other species.

Even with genetic engineering, the major factor steering evolution is still natural selection. The examples of rabbits and kudzu introduced into new environments are not directly applicable, since genetic engineering does not produce new species. It introduces novel variation into species. Since far more mutations and recombinations occur naturally than will ever occur through genetic engineering, and since the real factor in *steering* the course of evolution is *selection*, not mutation, the impact of genetic engineering will always be dwarfed by these natural processes. Certainly, genetic engineering now adds "artificial recombination, as a potential source of added variation. But selection is the main directive force in evolution" (Davis 1977, p. 554). Indeed, we affect natural selection significantly through our impact on environments. Anything that we engineer genetically will be sifted by the winnowing fork of natural selection, and almost inevitably it will be cast off as nonviable or nonadaptive.

What is the significance of genetic engineering for evolution? It is not in the impact of genetic engineering upon the course of evolution. Rather, it lies in the evolution of genetic engineering itself. If another species were to evolve the capacity to direct mutations, either in itself or in other species, we would regard that a momentous breakthrough in the course of evolution. Recall the comment of Bernard Davis that the course of evolution would have been much slower if it were not for the evolution of natural recombination agents such as viruses (Davis 1980, p. 79). Once, in the distant past, there evolved a relationship between organic molecules and organisms that permitted the exchange of genetic material outside lines of descent. Now, in our time, there has evolved a way for one species to *use* these same molecules and organisms to exchange genetic material, across lines of descent, according to preconceived intentions. The first evolutionary event occurred in biological evolution and vastly increased its speed and potentiality. The second evolutionary event, the discovery of genetic engineering, is occurring in our cultural evolution and introduces the factor of conscious intentionality at the microbiological level.

Before genetic engineering, the microbiological processes by which genetic material is exchanged across species took place without benefit to any particular species or classification of organisms. In this sense, natural recombination was value-free: No biological group benefited more than any other. The whole front of evolutionary change was assisted. The availability of mutations was not prejudiced. Genetic engineering changes this. Mutations now are skewed, ever so slightly, in favor of our own kind.

Far more important than each new use of this technology is the *technology itself*. Through it, we human beings now act quickly, precisely, and directly on genetic material. This is new in the history of evolution and new in human culture. Evolution, of course, is still steered by natural selection, and it is doubtful that our genetic engineering, significant though it is, will redirect evolution's course or unleash some great and terrible new creature. But we will contribute something new, even if it is something small. Exactly how much novelty we introduce is not the point. What is important is that a creature, *homo sapiens*, has discovered a way to introduce conscious intentionality into genetic recombination. This creature must now ask: to what end?

3

The Purpose of Genetic Engineering

Like any technology, genetic engineering exists to serve certain purposes. This is such an obvious characteristic of technology that we rarely bother to ask what purposes our technologies are intended to serve. Failure to ask this question, however, may have unfortunate consequences. "Can we, dare we, rest content with an approach to the world which gives us the techniques to modify it at will, while giving us no clues as to how it should be modified, except the dangerous facts of our own desires?" (Ward 1982, p. 112).

What is the purpose of genetic engineering? Some will suggest that its purpose is to benefit human beings. Others will suggest that its purpose is to benefit nature, which is probably understood as life on earth. I will suggest that the purpose of genetic engineering is to expand our ability to participate in God's work of redemption and creation and thereby to glorify God. In saying this, I am not saying that genetic engineering should not be used to benefit humans or nature, but that the full meaning of human and natural benefit is found in the attempt to glorify and serve God. In order to say why this is so, we must first examine the suggestions that this technology be used either to benefit humans or to benefit nature.

For the Benefit of Humanity

By contributing to health care, agriculture, energy, mining, and a host of other activities, genetic engineering will make life better for human beings. So great is its potential human benefit that some will say that the purpose of the technology is to benefit humanity. Our point is not so much to dispute the claim that genetic engineering will benefit humans as to clarify some of its limitations.

There is nothing sinister about the suggestion that genetic engineering will be used for the benefit of human beings. For example, a 1986 statement on genetic engineering by the National Council of Churches is entitled "Genetic Science for Human Benefit" (National Council of the Churches of Christ 1986). While genetic engineering does entail certain risks, it is becoming widely agreed that, with proper safeguards, the potential benefits outweigh the potential risks. This leads us to ask, Is genetic engineering to be developed, at great effort and expense, *because* of its potential benefit to humans? Does the human benefit justify the technology? Is human benefit the criterion by which we decide the merits of each line of research? While there is no question that genetic engineering will benefit humans, it is important that we think as clearly as we can about what we mean by human benefit. At least five problems arise when we try to say that the purpose of genetic engineering is human benefit.

The Problem of Shortsightedness

As we have seen, many of the unintended, negative consequences of agriculture have occurred as by-products of intentional efforts to improve agriculture. Limited knowledge of ecology meant that our ancestors were unable to predict the impact of their farming techniques. Fortunately, genetic engineering comes to us in the context of contemporary biology, which now includes ecology. While this does not give us much greater ability to predict the consequences of our actions, it does make us aware that our actions can, in time, lead to consequences that are the opposite of what we intended.

While the dangerous, unintended consequences of agriculture have taken millennia to accumulate, the consequences of genetic engineering, both intended and unintended, will arise more quickly. The speed of genetic engineering, in comparison to traditional selective breeding, is crucial in this regard. The concern we face, then, is that in the pursuit of genetic engineering for human benefit, short-term benefits will be won at the expense of long-term costs, many of which may be unintended and unforeseen. Any particular application of genetic engineering may be beneficial for humans in the short run but damaging in the long run to the environment upon which we depend.

The Problem of Who Shall Benefit

Genetic engineering does not simply bring greater health or comfort to those who use its products. It brings prestige and wealth to those who discover a gene or develop a therapy. This is not inappropriate, but it must be recognized in any candid discussion of the human benefits of genetic engineering. Weighing the needs of the hungry or of the chronically ill against the desire for fame or wealth is no academic question. Priorities for corporate and institutional research are determined by just such deliberation (Lappe 1984). What exactly will determine the uses of this technology? What benefits will be most influential in directing priorities for research?

The Problem of Anthropocentrism

Recently the Western tradition has been criticized as being anthropocentric (Gustafson 1981, 1984). By this it is meant that not only are we each egocentric but also, collectively, our values are centered upon ourselves as a species. Even when we are altruistic, our concern for others stops with other humans. Other species are valuable only in reference to their usefulness to us. Anthropocentrism, then, is the tendency to value the nonhuman only in reference to human use or enjoyment. At its worst, it treats other species as mere objects. Genetic engineering will act, inevitably, on other creatures. If this technology is intended to serve humans, are there any limits to what it will do to other species? Human benefit might be a basis for arguing for some protection and regard for other species, since they have aesthetic, recreational, commercial, and ecological value to us. But if their value is grounded only in their value to us, then there are few meaningful limits to what we might do with them. With genetic engineering, we will not only continue to *use* other species, we will make them *more usable*. There will always be technological limits to our ability to change other species so that they are more useful. But will there be any moral or religious restraints that will recognize the value of the nonhuman creation beyond its value to us?

The Problem of Human Uniqueness

The philosophical distinction between human and nonhuman, upon which the whole notion of human benefit rests, is undermined by work in genetics. In the Western philosophical and religious tradition, the distinction between the human and the nonhuman was grounded on the claim that the human person is a soul, metaphysically distinct from the nonhuman creation. Genetics research, however, shows correlations between genes and personality. These correlations seriously undermine the notion that the personal and the nonpersonal are metaphysically distinct realities.

Furthermore, in the distant future, it may become possible to make genetic alterations in the personality of future humans. Whether or not this is wise cannot be decided in reference to the criterion of human benefit, since the action would change the criterion itself!

The Problem of Conflicting Human Purposes

When we speak of genetic engineering as a benefit to *humanity*, we make it sound as if humanity were a single entity capable of deciding what it wants. There is no coherent human purpose, only a welter of conflicting purposes. For example, one science writer observed that researchers in livestock genetics had the goal of "seeking the genes that control fat deposition in cattle, so they can get a leaner steak on the U.S. market and a fattier one on the Japanese market" (Roberts 1990a, p. 550). Sometimes, we can find ways to pursue our purposes in cooperation with others, and contracts are formed. But more often our purposes conflict with those of others, and competition ensues. It is impossible to speak of a human purpose or a human benefit. We can speak of personal benefit or corporate benefit, and perhaps of national benefit. But even in the case of a national benefit, how is a nation to decide what it wants? An election comes closest to what we might call a national decision-making process. Even here, we are using the term "decision" as an anthropomorphic metaphor, projecting on the body politic (to extend the metaphor) the capability of thought and decision making.

Through the conflict of individual and corporate purposes, an economic and social order emerges. But we should not think that this order represents a decision of humanity, or that it lies in the best interest of the species as a whole. There is no "invisible hand," such as Adam Smith postulated, that harmonizes conflicting interests. "A complex system like an ecology or a market economy cannot have a goal in the sense that a single individual can, and any attempt to impose one leads to disaster" (Barrow and Tipler 1986, pp. 141–42).

This leads us to conclude that since genetic engineering involves nations, corporations, individual researchers, investors, and consumers, it cannot be said to serve the interests of humanity. It may very well serve the interests of human beings, but not of humanity, simply because there is no way in which the interests of the species can be determined. We must expect, then, that genetic engineering applications, far from being beneficial to all humanity, will benefit some, not all. While it might be a noble aspiration to intend that this technology benefit all, this goal is impossible except to those who think they can decide what benefits humanity as a whole.

But surely, someone might say, a vaccine against malaria would benefit humanity unambiguously. If put on a global ballot, how could it fail to win overwhelming approval? But this goal of a malaria vaccine has failed to attract major corporate interest. Because of the incoherence of the processes by which we humans determine what is in our best interests, something as obviously beneficial as a malaria vaccine fails to become a priority.

For the Benefit of Nature

One way to try to avoid these problems is to recognize nature as valuable in its own right, over and beyond its usefulness to human beings. Nature as a whole, not just human beings, would then be seen as the beneficiary of genetic engineering. In examining this proposal, our goal will not be to entirely reject the suggestion that nature can benefit from genetic engineering. Rather, we will examine this suggestion critically to see if it can bear the weight of justifying this technology and defining its uses.

We will approach this question in two ways. First, we will ask the broad question of whether evolution as a whole exhibits progress. If it does exhibit progress, then it could be argued that genetic engineering should be used to enhance that progress. Second, we will turn to the much narrower question of whether individual organisms and organs exhibit purpose. If they have a purpose, then it could be said that genetic engineering should be used to remove obstacles that keep them from their purpose.

It has been argued that nature is progressing toward greater diversity and complexity of living things. The theory of evolution, it has been said, reveals this. Because nature progresses, human beings (who are part of this evolutionary progress and owe their existence to it) ought to contribute to this progress (Waddington 1941 [1948], J. Huxley 1943 [1947]).

Does nature, in fact, exhibit progress? The suggestion that there is progress in nature is fairly recent. The idea of progress grew out of the Christian view of history. In contrast to cyclical views, early Christian thinkers emphasized the one-time character of major events of creation and redemption. The fall, they said, put history in motion toward a great consummation. This view of history as movement toward a goal, when secularized in the eighteenth century, became the modern idea of progress (Becker 1932). Enlightenment philosophy and science were seen as the motive force of this progress. "To the future the Philosophers looked, as to a promised land, a new millennium" (Becker 1932, p. 118).

In Darwin's generation this idea of progress was applied to nature. Prior to the study of geology in the early 1800s, nature was assumed to be static. Geology and then biology, of course, changed this. Nature was seen as dynamic and changing. The question then arose: Were nature's changes progressive? Was nature itself moving toward a better state? On the surface, the whole idea of organic evolution, from simple forms to complex organisms, seems to establish the fact of natural progress beyond reasonable doubt.

Julian Huxley argued that Darwin's theory of evolution opens a new understanding of natural progress (J. Huxley 1943 [1947]). Our duty as humans, now that we are aware of this progress in nature, is to conform to it and to enhance its movement. At about the same time as Huxley, the biologist C. H. Waddington sought to distance Darwinian evolution from Nazi ideology, but he advocated the adoption of "the scientific attitude . . . whose final standard of value is an observed process of evolutionary advance" (1941 [1948], p. 172). A similar position was taken more recently by V. L. Parsegian: "Taking lessons from the long evolutionary strivings of the past, reason demands that a primary purpose of man be the maintenance of conditions that assure his own survival and that assure evolutionary progression" (1973, p. 242).

What accounts for this faith in "evolutionary progression"? It may derive from the idea of natural selection. This is a powerful concept in evolutionary biology, but it is an anthropomorphic metaphor, as Darwin himself no doubt realized. As human breeders select, so nature selects. Since human breeders select with an intention of progress, so (it is assumed, through an improper extension of the metaphor) nature selects intentionally for progress. Darwin himself could write, "Man selects only for his own good; Nature only for that of the being which she tends" (1968 [1859], p. 132). If taken literally, the metaphor of "natural selection" is dangerously misleading. It evokes the idea that nature is a conscious agent, guiding a process so that it is progressive.

Not all evolutionary biologists, of course, agree that evolution is morally progressive. Fifty years before Sir Julian's proclamation of evolutionary progress, T. H. Huxley (1947 [1893]) came to the opposite conclusion. After a recital of the results of recent studies of animal (including primate) behavior, George Williams comments, "Huxley viewed the cosmic process as an enemy that must be combated. Mine is a similar but more extreme position, based on the more extreme contemporary view of natural selection as a process for maximizing selfishness" (1988, p. 399).

The fact that leading biologists disagree leads us to ask whether this is a question that will be resolved by further research in the field. Regarding the conflict between T. H. and Julian Huxley, Stephen Toulmin comments, "Can we choose between their views? Not on scientific grounds; for the question, whether social and moral progress are to be regarded as a continuation of the process of natural selection or as a reaction against it, is not one which can be answered by appeal to observation or experiments" (1970 [1957], pp. 48–49). Further developments in biology cannot be expected to resolve the debate because the issue under discussion is not a question of biology, according to Toulmin. Rather, it is a question of what he calls "scientific myth"—scientific in that it begins with scientific theory, but myth in that it goes far beyond theory to issues of morality. "The idea of a Sovereign Order of Nature is, in other words, not a purely biological idea: it is an idea originating in biology, but taken over from it and extended to do a fresh, non-biological job" (Toulmin 1970 [1957], p. 39).

Ian Barbour extends the criticism of attempts to move from evolutionary biology to morality. Any such attempt "fails, we submit, to answer unambiguously the two questions: *what is the direction of evolution,* and *why should man imitate it?*" (1966, p. 413). Evolution, Barbour continues, has been claimed as a support for virtually every ideology. The values that are supposedly found in evolution come, in fact, from the Western tradition and are read into evolution by those who seek scientific support for their perspective (Barbour 1966, p. 403).

These critiques by Toulmin and Barbour are helpful in sorting out the dangers of drawing moral implications from evolutionary biology. But they go too far in divorcing biology from morality. The evolution and organization of living things strike us, deeply and intuitively, as valuable, and the value of this process imposes an obligation to any organism that is part of this process and capable of discerning its value.

The science of biology is the means through which we humans try to understand the evolution and organization of living things. If there is value in this evolution and organization, biology should shed some light on it. The fact that T. H. and Julian Huxley disagreed so sharply should not deter us from continuing to ask, Are there moral values in nature, and can we know them? More specifically, can we discern in biological evolution a moral progress that places obligations upon humans? Does the study of nature disclose anything of moral significance that is inherent within nature, as opposed to something read into the data by the human investigator?

Contemporary evolutionary theorists have revisited the question of purpose in evolution. A current textbook on evolution defines evolutionary progress this way: "Progress, then, may be defined as *systematic change in a feature belonging to all members of a sequence in such a way that posterior members of the sequence exhibit an improvement of that feature.* More simply, progress may be defined as a directional change for the better" (Dobzhansky, Ayala, Stebbins, et al. 1977, p. 508; emphasis in original). In the view of the authors, the claim that evolution is progressive has two parts. First, evolution must be a directional change. Second, this change must be marked by an increase in value as assessed by a nonanthropocentric standard. The directional change can be established quantitatively, but the increase of value involves a moral or at least an aesthetic judgment. "The notion of progress requires that a value judgment be made of what is better and what is worse" (Ayala 1974; Dobzhansky, Ayala, Stebbins, et al. 1977, p. 508).

In asking whether evolution exhibits an increase in value, Ayala (1974) and Dobzhansky et al. (1977) make two helpful distinctions. First, they distinguish between uniform progress and net progress. Uniform progress involves constant improvement, while net progress only requires that final members of a sequence show improvement on average over initial members. The second distinction is between general and particular progress, general involving the entire evolutionary process and particular involving some sequences or some time periods and excluding others. Ayala and Dobzhansky argue that "there is no standard according to which *uniform* progress can be said to have occurred in the evolution of life" (Dobzhansky, Ayala, Stebbins, et al. p. 1977, p. 511; cf. Ayala 1974, pp. 342–43). Evolutionary dead ends and mass extinctions preclude the possibility of uniform progress.

Is there any standard, however, by which we might say that net general progress has occurred? Various standards or criteria have been suggested, among them an increase in the total amount of genetic information. This is difficult to assess, since a great deal of the DNA in modern organisms (including ourselves) may be repetitive or nonsense. Another proposed standard is the expansion of life. This might mean several things, such as the growth in the number of species, the number of organisms, the mass of living matter, or the total rate of energy flow (Dobzhansky, Ayala, Stebbins, et al. 1977, p. 511). Ambiguities arise in the attempt to apply these criteria to the history of evolution, although a strong argument might be made that net progress has occurred in evolution (at least to the present) when assessed by any of these standards.

Ayala suggests that "increased ability to gather and process information" be taken as the standard for progress (1974, p. 349). This ability aids organisms in adapting to their environment, and therefore it is a legitimate criterion when judged on evolutionary (as opposed to anthropocentric) grounds. When all species are evaluated by this criterion, humans are clearly the most advanced. "Man is by this measure of biological progress the most progressive organism on the planet" (Ayala 1974, p. 352). Dobzhansky et al. (1977) note, "[This] is an acceptable criterion of progress because it illuminates certain features of the evolution of life. However, it is not necessarily better or worse than other criteria of progress. . . . By certain criteria, flowering plants are more progressive than many animals" (Dobzhansky, Ayala, Stebbins, et al. 1977, p. 516). It appears that we need a criterion for evaluating criteria of biological progress.

One of the more striking features of this ambiguity is that criteria seem inevitably to favor one species (or family) at the expense of others. "What is progression from the point of view of one species would be retrogression from the view of another. Human beings tend to take an anthropocentric position, and regard any development which leads to human characteristics as progressive, and any other line of development as either retrogressive or neutral" (Barrow and Tipler 1986, p. 129).

Furthermore, if ability to process information is regarded as the best criterion, then a paradox emerges. The ability to process information requires a large brain, but this increases risk at childbirth and involves a far greater parental investment, decreasing reproductive rates. "Intelligence has no *a priori* advantage, but it is a clear and unmistakable reproductive hazard" (Barrow and Tipler 1986, p. 131). In primates, and especially in the lineage leading to humans, "unusual feeding strategies and locomotion" combined to create a situation in which natural selection could favor increased encephalization (Barrow and Tipler 1986, p. 131). The paradox here is that if ability to process information is progressive, nature typically selects against progress!

From all this we conclude, first, that progress in nature is ambiguous, and second, that any moral obligation placed upon human beings is equally ambiguous. We cannot say, then, that genetic engineering should be used to serve evolutionary progress, because we do not know whether there is any such progress or how we would recognize it.

Whether further scientific understanding will remove some of the ambiguity is an interesting question. As we noted, Toulmin does not think it will. In our discussion, we have recognized a greater role for science in discerning value than has Toulmin. It may be that future science will be more helpful on the question of the morality (or immorality, as the case may be) of evolution. However, the Christian idea of nature as disordered creation, as we will develop it, will lead us to expect that future scientific insight will only fill in greater details of the moral ambiguity of the evolutionary process, portraying it as a process of great creativity and wonder, yet of horrific violence and self-interest. The moral ambiguity—the chaotic mixture of good and bad—will not disappear with further knowledge, but we will understand it in greater detail and depth. The ambiguity does not lie ultimately in our knowledge, as limited as it is. Unresolved moral ambiguity lies in nature itself.

We need now to consider briefly the second question, namely, whether nature, at more limited or local levels, exhibits purpose. If so, then it is at least possible to speak of genetic engineering being used to assist these limited or local purposes.

The answer to the question must be yes, for the simple reason that we humans, who are biological or natural organisms, experience ourselves acting with a purpose in mind, and account for the behavior of other persons this way. In ordinary speech, we describe animal behavior with reference to an explanatory purpose, saying that birds migrate to avoid harsh weather, or that the eye's purpose is to see. Some biologists, in a desire to avoid what they take to be Aristotelian teleological explanations, try to eliminate references to purpose from biology. Others, more in agreement with Aristotle, point out that reference to purpose is unavoidable, but that our referring to a purpose does not commit us to belief in a designer. Saying that the purpose of an eye is seeing does not mean that a designer intended to make an organ capable of vision. The eye came into existence, in perhaps as many as forty separate lineages, as a result of natural selection, even though natural selection itself is a nonpurposive process of selective retention of random mutations. Even if a designer is excluded from the general process, purpose may be retained in biology when we speak of the organs and the organisms evolved through that process.

Embryological development is another example of purposive action in biology. A fertilized egg, in spite of minor variations in the environment, develops into a bird or a human being according to an inherent design. "The development of an egg into a chicken, or of a human zygote into a human being, are examples of determinate natural teleological processes" (Dobzhansky, Ayala, Stebbins, et al. 1977, p. 500). DNA is the material basis for this natural teleological or purposive process.

Because of genetic engineering, embryological development is the most interesting example of purpose or teleological process in biology. Through genetic engineering, we can alter the genetic code that guides this purposive process. When we do so, are we countering natural purpose? If we are removing a known defective gene, or supplying a gene that is normally found in the species and is necessary to health, then we could easily say that we are cooperating with natural purpose. This would be based on prior knowledge of a normal genome for the species and on the assumption that the normal is what is *really* natural— that "defects" are somehow unnatural, even though they are the products of natural processes. All this becomes more ambiguous when we think of using genetic engineering to enhance the traits of organisms. Do we enhance or defy natural purpose when we try to insert a gene for added growth hormone into the fertilized egg of a farm animal, or a gene to allow nitrogen fixation into wheat?

The evolutionary process has been alternatively portrayed as moral, amoral, and immoral, and we humans have been urged to cooperate with it, ignore it, or resist it, respectively. Local or limited purposes conflict or are ambiguous in their claims. On the one hand, nature seems to permit no interference; any technology is unnatural and therefore immoral. On the other hand, we and our technology are part of nature; any technology is therefore natural and acceptable. This leads us to conclude that when we claim that genetic engineering should be used to serve nature, it is not at all clear what we are saying. We land ourselves in hopeless ambiguities when we attempt to defend and (more important) to limit genetic engineering by what we think cooperates with nature's own progress and purpose.

In the Service of God

Stephen Toulmin, paraphrasing Julian Huxley, wrote, "God has failed: we must therefore put our trust in Evolution, and vary our ethical beliefs as it directs" (Toulmin 1970 [1957], p. 51). Our conclusion, reached in the previous section, is that evolution itself has failed. It has produced us but cannot direct us. Nature will not guide us in the right way to act on nature; evolution will not direct our redirection of evolution.

Individually, however, our actions upon nature are not directionless. We each act according to our own purpose. Whether the goal of our action is to help others or to benefit ourselves, to feed the hungry or to gain a competitive advantage over another corporation or another nation, we each act to achieve ends. Some will argue that in the global cacophony of human actions, a kind of order emerges. The free market of conflicting interests is guided by an invisible hand that orders the chaos to the benefit of the whole, even if not always to the immediate good of each individual. But just as there is no designer in evolution, in spite of the appearance of progress, there is no invisible hand guiding our economy, our culture, or our symbiotic relationship with other species. We are on our own: No invisible hand will reconcile our conflicting interests or undo our damage. We cannot trust in the wisdom of nature to save us, for nature is blind and purposeless. Nature does not care about us.

Nor will Christian theology offer us a God who will serve us by saving us. If our symbiotic relationship with other species continues in a direction that is dangerous ultimately to ourselves, no God will rescue us. If we use genetic engineering to accelerate these trends, no God will reverse them. We cannot appeal to God to save us from selfishness and shortsightedness. The God who saves is the God who is served.

In an age of rapid technological advance, God is not needed to protect us from nature so much as to protect us from misguided technology. According to biologist Arnold W. Ravin, "the proper mission of religion . . . is to help man find meaning and motivation for his participation in an evolution over which he has no certain guidance or final control"; he goes on to comment, "I understand the awful charge I am conferring upon religion, for I am aware how fraught with difficulty are the questions related to the origin and validation of moral values" (1977, p. 36). So we now come to this difficult religious question: What is our human purpose, and how shall we use this technology? In putting the questions this way, we are no longer asking about the purpose of our technology. We are asking now about the purpose of humanity itself within the scheme of creation.

With elegant simplicity, the Westminster Shorter Catechism asks, as its first question, about the purpose or end of humanity. To the question, "What is the chief end of man?" the proper answer is "Man's chief end is to glorify God, and to enjoy him forever" (The Shorter Catechism, Q. 1). The catechism paraphrases the text from Paul: "Whatever you do, do all to the glory of God" (1 Corinthians 10:31b, RSV). Human beings do not exist to gratify or to serve themselves but to glorify and enjoy their Creator.

Everything exists for the glory of God. God is the maker of all things, and they have their value in reference to God, not in reference to themselves or to humans. This applies especially to human beings: Our value is no greater than our value to God. But it applies to all things: Their value is not less than their value to God. So when we act upon ourselves, upon other humans, and upon other creatures, we measure the legitimacy and the limits of our actions not by whether we benefit ourselves but by whether we glorify God.

The God disclosed in the life and ministry of Jesus is especially concerned for the weak, the sick, and the poor. One of the problems of basing our moral standards on the evolutionary process is that this process seems to disregard the individual, especially the weak or the one who is less fit for survival in the environment. Evolutionary progress in a particular species occurs through the nonselection of the less fit individuals in the population of that species. To base one's life on the example of Jesus, however, means to be concerned especially about the welfare of the poor and the weak, to give priority to their needs, and to preserve their place in the community of the human species, thereby reversing natural selection by favoring the retention of their genes.

Christian ethics measures moral progress by the treatment given to the weakest or poorest members of the human community. Genetic engineering, when legitimated and limited by Christian faith, would be used primarily to serve the needs of the weak, the sick, and the poor. This conviction should have a direct impact on the selection of research priorities and on the development of flexible marketing arrangements, so that the benefits of this technology will be readily available to those who need them most.

To live and work for the glory of God means to place personal benefit at a lower level of importance. It is to renounce the use of power for personal aggrandizement, seeking instead to use power for the service of others. It is to seek to participate in the redemptive and creative work of God.

4

Responding to the New Situation

Since the mid-1960s, a number of theologians and ethicists have responded to developments in genetics research. These writers have recognized the religious significance of genetic engineering. They agree that such a significant change in our relationship with creation will bring with it a profound change in our relationship with the Creator.

We will summarize the views of six theologians. Karl Rahner, Paul Ramsey, and Robert Brungs, who are discussed first, are apprehensive about the directions in which this new technology might take us. Roger Shinn, J. Robert Nelson, and Hans Schwarz, by contrast, mix caution with a greater openness to the important benefits that this technology promises.

After summarizing the views of these theologians, we will turn to the statements of ecumenical and denominational bodies, concluding with a brief summary of the major themes that have emerged to date in the church's effort to respond to developments in genetics.

The Response of Theologians

Karl Rahner

The earliest and in some respects the most thoughtful theological engagement with genetic engineering is that of Karl Rahner, who published two essays in the late 1960s in anticipation of later developments. In these essays, Rahner asks about the theological significance of a range of newer technologies that affect not only individual human beings but also humanity as a whole. Among these technologies are new ways to make genetic changes.

Rahner uses the phrase "genetic manipulation" for a range of anticipated technologies. He seems to have artificial insemination by donor (AID) most specifically in mind. He appears to be convinced that genetic manipulation of some sort would produce a "group of test-tube men, whose intelligence quotients would be clearly considerably higher from birth" (Rahner 1966b, p. 247). Despite the unfortunate fact that Rahner's writings preceded the actual development of what we now know as genetic engineering, the quality of his theology as a whole is such that his comments are highly instructive.

Should human beings shape or manipulate their own future? Rahner's first consideration is surprisingly affirmative: "According to Christian anthropology man really is the being who manipulates himself. . . . Man, as the being who is free in relation to God, is in a most radical way empowered to do what he wills with himself, freely able to align himself towards his own ultimate goals" (Rahner 1966a, p. 212). In more classic philosophic terms, the human essence is open to our own defining. "When his essence *is* complete it is as he himself has freely created it" (Rahner 1966a, p. 213).

Rahner observes that it is very difficult to proceed here theologically by reasoning from nature or from ontological categories. What is essential to human nature? "At this point the theologian who proceeds by means of ontological categories finds himself in severe difficulties, for there is little, indeed almost nothing, in man's biological constitution which he can recognise as necessary to his nature" (Rahner 1966b, p. 232). This very openness of human beings to self-manipulation, however, is the ground of Rahner's concern. He observes that human self-manipulation sets us upon a "one-way, irreversible historical course," forcing those who come later to live with our mistakes (Rahner 1966a, p. 218). The traditional Christian doctrine of "the fall" and of original sin affirms precisely this point: Self-manipulation is irreversible. We should guard against the illusion that we can undo our self-manipulative errors. History, Rahner argues, is one way. If we were to lock our present historic choices in our genetic code, future generations would have a less free future than we have.

Even more basic, however, is Rahner's insistence that while we human beings define and create our own essence, we enter upon this task from a givenness (or *existentiale)* that must be accepted. We "must accept this particular *existentiale* as well as the task of self-determination" (Rahner 1966b, p. 243). While the theme of self-determination might appear to lead in the direction of a highly positive stance toward genetic intervention, the theme of the givenness of the individual human *existentiale* leads in the opposite direction, for what is given is precisely the mystery of our genetic makeup at birth. We must accept this givenness with gratitude, not with fear or with the desire to change it for ourselves or our offspring. "Genetic manipulation is the embodiment of the fear of oneself, the fear of accepting one's self as the unknown quantity it is" (Rahner 1966b, p. 245). He continues: "What, in actual fact, is the driving force behind genetic manipulation? What sort of person is driven to it? And the answer would be, in the first place, the *hate* of one's destiny; and secondly, it is the man who, at his innermost level, is in despair because he cannot *dispose* of existence" (Rahner 1966b, p. 245).

Human givenness is safeguarded because the genetic origin of each human individual lies in the intimacy of sexual union, and for Rahner this means a decisive aversion to artificial insemination, because it is a technological intrusion upon the sexual intimacy of marriage and because genetic material foreign to the married couple is introduced. "Genetic manipulation, however, does two things: it fundamentally separates the marital union from the procreation of a new person as this permanent embodiment of the unity of married love; and it transfers procreation, isolated and torn from its human matrix, to an area outside man's sphere of intimacy" (Rahner 1966b, p. 246).

Yet "Christianity is the religion of the absolute future" (Rahner 1966a, p. 219). Through our efforts, indeed through the dynamics of the whole creation, the creation moves in history toward its destiny. We ourselves participate in the definition of that destiny. God, who is absolute, mysterious, and transcendent, defines creation's destiny by acting in and through the creation itself. "For Christianity acknowledges the absolute, infinite God who is superior to the world, a radical and infinite mystery, as the God who in free grace communicates himself in his absolute mystery as its innermost principle and ultimate future, who sustains and drives history as his genuinely most intimate concern, not only distinguishing himself from it as its creator" (Rahner 1966a, p. 219). As intimate presence, God in grace both judges and confirms our efforts at self-definition. For the grace of God does not define us, but through grace God allows our self-definition, misguided and arrogant as it is, to be redeemed as God's own gift of human definition. In this sense, we participate in shaping the future by doing, but we also encounter the future by receiving. This receptivity or openness is consent to death:

> The arrival of this future occurs essentially in the act of death. . . . One only reaches the absolute future by way of death's zero hour, not because the former is death's gift, not because it could be calculated to be impossible in any other way, but because, beyond all deduction, absolute love was pleased to triumph in its greatest defeat. (Rahner 1966a, p. 220)

While Rahner is remarkably prescient of subsequent technological developments and of their implications for theology, and while his theology affirms the necessity of human self-transcendence, this self-transcendence occurs at a spiritual level rather than at the level of evolutionary biology. Biotechnology does not contribute to salvation. Rather, this technology interferes with the creative graciousness of our genetic inheritance, a grace that must be accepted, not altered, for the acceptance of grace is the condition of any salvation.

Paul Ramsey

In the earliest days of genetic engineering, Paul Ramsey engaged some of its advocates with a serious and thought-provoking challenge. In *Fabricated Man*, Ramsey (1970) argues against those who advocate wide-ranging uses of the emerging genetic techniques as a way to take charge of the human future. He does not object to medical applications, but the effort to improve humanity in general (as opposed to the individual patient) sparks his concern.

One technique to which Ramsey objects is artificial insemination with donor sperm (AID). Ramsey criticizes this as "the first breach" in the integrity of human parenthood (Ramsey 1970, p. 133). Even with a technique as well intentioned as AID, an assault has been made upon the biological integrity of humanity, human love, and human procreation. "When the transmission of life has been debiologized, human parenthood as a created covenant of life is placed under massive assault and men and women will no longer be who they are" (Ramsey 1970, p. 135). It turns procreation into reproduction, a technological process rather than an intimate, biological one, Ramsey cautions.

More important, AID transgresses a basic theological limit. "Men ought not to play God before they learn to be men, and after they have learned to be men they will not play God" (Ramsey 1970, p. 138). In particular, Ramsey warns against the shallow optimism of those who advocate "playing God" with the emerging genetic technology. For human beings to become their own creators and to determine their own biological destiny, Ramsey believes, is to open the way to human destruction. "Man becoming his own self-creator raises far more than vague religious trepidations. . . . It is not Christianity alone but man as well that the revolutionary biologists have left behind in their flights of grasping after godhead" (Ramsey 1970, pp. 144–45). For Ramsey, this "surrogate theology" of the revolutionary biologists removes all restraints and lets loose a "technological imperative": "The immanent providence of a morally blind biological technology decrees, of course, that men-gods *must* do what they *can* do" (Ramsey 1970, p. 149; emphasis in original). Against this prospect, Ramsey argues, we should and must revolt, demanding that there are things we can do that we must not do, that there are limits that must be respected, and that there are compelling reasons to leave the human future to the uncertainties of nature than to the decisions of a "minority of scientific saviors" (Ramsey 1970, p. 151).

Robert Brungs

Human beings cannot be nontechnological, Robert Brungs, S.J., argues. Even our preagricultural ancestors used technology to alter their environment. In our time, the pace of technological change has accelerated. Until genetic engineering, however, the purpose of technology was to alter the environment, making it more liveable or beneficial. Genetic engineering, Brungs argues, is unlike all previous technology. "In the classical technologies the end was the changing of the environment external to the human, either the physical or social environment, for the perceived betterment of human beings. The biological technologies do not look so much to the betterment of humans as they do to 'better humans' " (Brungs 1983, p. 279). In the past it was not always clear what making a better world might have meant; now it is even less clear what it means to make a better human. Even medical technology, which treats the human subject, only aims at restoring health or reducing pain, not at enhancing the traits of individuals and their descendants. Therefore, "The major issue is what, indeed, is a better human?" (Brungs 1983, p. 279).

Brungs fears that any definition of "a better human" will be warped by ideological and social pressures. The power of genetic techniques to reduce chance or randomness in human conception, he argues, is really the power to replace grace with control. "The principal reason for any social application of biotechnologies is more order, less randomness, in the human situation" (Brungs 1983, p. 281). Somewhat surprisingly, however, Brungs acknowledges that there are important and legitimate benefits to biotechnology. So he asks, "Will we have the wisdom, will we acquire the wisdom to use it to our true benefit?" (Brungs 1983, p. 283).

J. Robert Nelson

a certain dumme guennen (Rahner)

Nelson argues that all of the current public debates about genetic engineering are religious questions, at least in part. These debates do not belong exclusively to religious thought, but religious thinking should enter explicitly into the discussion because religious issues are inevitably implicit in the basic assumptions made by all parties in the debate.

Basic to Nelson's approach to theology and genetic engineering is the belief that human beings are each individually created in the image of God. "Faith in the 'image of God' as the mold in which human beings are cast fundamentally determines the moral stance of both Jews and Christians" (Nelson 1984, p. 157). Upon this basis, human distinctiveness (from the rest of creation), human dignity, and infinite personal human value are grounded. Christians have no comprehensive ready-made theology to apply to the questions posed by genetic engineering, but Christians generally agree on the centrality of the *imago dei* motif, Nelson argues.

Furthermore, Nelson identifies several basic Christian theological themes that are important to a theological assessment of genetic engineering. His position could be summarized this way: The entire universe is a divine creation whose existence and order depend upon divine purpose and will. Among creatures, human beings occupy a special place and have freedom to create. Yet human beings are biological organisms, belonging to the earth and to the family of living things. Each person possesses a personal center or personhood to which the term "soul" or "spirit" might be applied.

Personally and collectively, human beings are created to live in relationship with their Creator. The value of each person and of all humanity depends upon this relationship; human dignity or worth is conferred upon us by our Creator. Each person should live life as a loan from God and therefore in reference to God's purposes, Nelson argues.

Human beings are free moral agents and are responsible for their lives and for their impact on the natural world. Violation of this moral responsibility is sin, "the inexplicable, demonic contradiction within each reasoning and willing person between the will to be good and do good on the one hand, and the disposition toward egoism and exclusive self-interest on the other. Sin is self-deception . . . [and] belongs to human societies at large" (Nelson 1984, p. 163). Recognizing the power of sin, Christians are skeptical about the pretenses of human good or the capacity of human reason to be free of self-centered prejudice. "What biblically based faith contributes is called 'the hermeneutics of suspicion' about human fallibility, self-confidence, and arrogance" (Nelson 1990, p. 46). Yet at the same time, Christians are willing to undertake risks because they know the future cannot be perfectly managed.

Above and beyond the suffering that sin brings, there is the suffering brought by natural calamities. This poses the question of God's justice, an ultimately insoluble problem according to Nelson. Christians learn to bear this inevitable suffering with patience, and even to suffer redemptively for and with others, as the cross signifies.

In applying these central themes of Christian theology to questions that arise from genetic engineering, Nelson sees no unusual theological or moral problem with genetically engineered pharmaceuticals or with human gene therapy. Even human germline research is challenged on technical grounds and out of scientific consideration (the unknown impact of future generations), not on theological grounds.

Roger Shinn

Few theologians or ethicists have participated in church discussions of genetic engineering as extensively as has Roger Shinn. Over two decades, he has been active in conversations held by the World Council of Churches, the National Council of the Churches of Christ, U.S.A., and the United Church of Christ. Accordingly, Shinn is particularly aware of the varying impact of technological change in different societies and in different regions of the globe.

In addition, Shinn recognizes that society, not technology or science, distinguishes good from bad, progress from problems. "It is society, not biology, that turns some genetic characteristics into liabilities" (Shinn 1982, p. 140). The moral vision of a society determines the ends that its technology serves. In earlier times, limited technology meant that less noble ends were only partly realized. "The more adept the human race becomes in technological skills, the more critical becomes the issue of its visions" (Shinn 1982, p. 140).

The moral vision of our technologically advanced society is a crucial concern. An ambiguity surrounds technology: The greater its benefits, the more worrisome its power. "I know no way of drawing a line and saying: thus far, scientific direction and control are beneficial; beyond this line they become destructive manipulation" (Shinn 1982, p. 142). There is no easy way to resolve the ambiguity or to avoid dealing with it. To avoid discussion and decision is, indeed, to decide. For Shinn, this is the logic of the "forced option," a logic that confronts us in many areas of technological change. The best that can be hoped for is a continued, thoughtful discussion that takes into account the richness of traditional moral and religious visions. Religious faith, in particular, nurtures the sense of purpose that is needed to guide a technologically advanced society. This faith is not some ancient wisdom uprooted from a primitive context and set down into a radically different present. Rather, it is the moral vision of religious traditions informed by the growing insights of science. How people respond to the challenges of the moment "will depend largely on their interests, their values, their faith. But purposeful action wants to be informed action" (Shinn 1982, p. 225). It is in a thoughtful, dialogical exchange between traditional religious morality and contemporary science and technology that Shinn sees some hope for the future.

Hans Schwarz

Finally, we consider the thought of German theologian Hans Schwarz. In an essay written at the very beginning of the age of what he calls "biogenetics," Schwarz identified a number of key theological themes, among them the inescapable value orientation of this emerging technology. This technology demands human decisions that are not purely technological but have more to do with art or the poetic. For Schwarz, this points to an "innermost relationship between all human activities" (Schwarz 1970, p. 259). Furthermore, genetic engineering raises questions of ends or goals, for its use requires that we ask what human ends or purposes it should serve.

Schwarz's view of genetic engineering is dependent upon an understanding of humanity as commissioned by God to participate in the continuing work of creation. "In Judeo-Christian faith man conceived himself for the first time as cooperator with God. He understands himself as being commissioned to cooperation with God in a positive way as technician and artist to fulfill the kingdom of God and to participate in the dominion of God over the earth" (Schwarz 1970, p. 262). When researchers and technicians see their work as cooperating with God's creative work, then God's purposes become the norm that defines human purpose. "In this function man is commissioned to pursue his intentions and activities in analogy to God's intention and activities by supporting and furthering them" (Schwarz 1970, p. 262).

Creation is not so much about origins, for Schwarz, as about the destiny or end of all things. God is creating now in anticipation of the consummation and perfection of creation. Consequently, for human beings to participate in the creative work of God means that we participate in God's transformation of the present into the new creation. For Schwarz, this is not some blind trust in technological progress as an end in itself. Such a trust can (and has) been profoundly disappointed, and we must be deeply concerned about the ways in which genetic engineering might dehumanize or destroy. The trust is grounded in the recognition that our technology can be used in the service of God's creative work toward a specific end, which Schwarz defines this way: "The good of the individual man as a God-responsive and God-responsible being, within the context of his life-preserving and pleasure-providing environment, must be the ultimate goal of all biogenetic progress" (Schwarz 1970, p. 263). For this reason, Schwarz argues that genetic engineering must not be left without a religious context. Rather, it must be incorporated into a "Judeo-Christian context," for this incorporation "would open the possibility in a positive way to understanding biogenetic progress as divine commission in analogy to God's creative and conserving actions" (Schwarz 1970, p. 264).

The Response of Churches

At every level, from the World Council of Churches to the local congregation, the church has attempted to respond corporately to developments in genetics. While cautious of abuses and wary of false optimism, the church positions we will consider are, for the most part, affirmative of the good that this technology can bring.

The World Council of Churches

Since 1969 the World Council of Churches (WCC) has reflected on the ethical and theological significance of biotechnology. In 1973 a consultation on "Genetics and the Quality of Life" was held, and its papers were published (World Council of Churches 1975). The WCC conference in 1979 on "Faith, Science and the Future" included a section on "Ethical Issues in the Biological Manipulation of Life."

In 1982 the WCC Working Committee on Church and Society released a report entitled "Manipulating Life: Ethical Issues in Genetic Engineering" (World Council of Churches 1982). This report noted that church responses to genetic engineering have often been based on fear and mistrust, but that these responses are frequently accompanied by "attempts to affirm even more strongly outdated doctrines of creation" (World Council of Churches 1982, p. 1). Unfortunately, the report does not offer an alternative doctrine.

Arguing for a holistic notion of the person, the report warns that "genetic manipulation amplifies and accelerates the tendency toward total reductionism" (World Council of Churches 1982, p. 8). This tendency is a dangerous threat to the very concept of humanness.

Genetic traits (such as skin color) are subject to societal prejudices. The emerging field of genetic engineering should not be allowed to provide a technological "solution" to racism or other forms of prejudice. "It is important to ask of every genetic proposal: what human purposes and desires does it project?" (World Council of Churches 1982, p. 9). The report worries about the kind of purposes governments might have for genetic research.

In July 1989 the Central Committee of the WCC approved the report "Biotechnology: Its Challenges to the Churches and the World" (World Council of Churches 1989). Among its recommendations, the report calls for a prohibition of the use of genetic testing for sex selection. It "stresses the need for pastoral counselling for individuals faced with difficult reproductive choices as well as personal and family decisions resulting from genetic information concerning themselves or others" (World Council of Churches 1989, p. 12). It asserts that "the patenting of life encodes into law a reductionist conception of life which seeks to remove any distinction between living and non-living things" (World Council of Churches 1989, p. 22), adding that "the integrity of creation is damaged if biotechnology is utilized by commercial pressures to manufacture new life forms that are valued only as economic commodities" (World Council of Churches 1989, p. 30). As a whole, the report takes a positive attitude toward genetic engineering and biotechnology. Its deepest reservations have to do with the corporate economic system in which research and development will occur. Apprehensive that genetic engineering will make those in wealthy nations more self-indulgent and those in poor nations more exploited, the report urges a transformation of the economic, political, and cultural context that surrounds the development of biotechnology.

The National Council of Churches

In 1980 a task force commissioned by the National Council of the Churches of Christ in the U.S.A. issued a report entitled "Human Life and the New Genetics." After assessing the ethical issues of current and prospective genetic technology, the task force devoted a brief chapter in the report to theological issues. They affirmed that life is a gift from God but that human beings are to show creativity in exploring life's possibilities. This creativity, however, has a double edge: On the one hand, it is the proper exercise of our God-given role to cultivate the garden of creation, but on the other hand, it tempts us "to build self-destructing towers of Babel" (National Council of Churches 1980, p. 41).

Christian tradition, the report continues, affirms that God works both through nature and through human action. God creates through nature, achieving divine purposes through natural process, yet without being identified with those processes. As God's creation, nature exhibits values that are inherently normative. Christians "have usually discerned some *Logos,* some creativity, some ordering principle that they could regard as normative. By contrast, they have often identified the 'unnatural' as wrong" (National Council of Churches 1980, p. 42). But God also acts through human beings, and at times intentional human acts interfere with the processes of nature to achieve a more moral outcome. "From this viewpoint 'the natural' may be less moral than the purposefully human act." Accordingly, "the effort to improve on nature is not inherently wrong" (National Council of Churches 1980, p. 42).

This leads to the somewhat confusing position that while God works through nature, God also works through human beings against nature. Or more precisely: God works through a part of nature (namely, human culture and technology) to redirect other parts of nature.

The report proceeds to raise questions about the impact of genetic engineering on human dignity. It notes that human beings are not subjects of scientific experimentation like other entities, but that a vastly higher probability of success must be anticipated before human subjects are used. "Human dignity upsets the conventional equations of cost and benefit" (National Council of Churches 1980, p. 44). Further, human dignity is not defined by any norm, genetic or otherwise, but all are regarded as equally and fully human, and the growing scientific sense of normal and abnormal in human genetics should not convince us otherwise.

Relieving suffering and forestalling death, the report notes, are humane acts and worthy of our best technical efforts. "Yet in the last analysis perhaps it is more important to know how to die than how to postpone death. Similarly, for humanity, there can be value in learning from suffering as well as in reducing suffering" (National Council of Churches 1980, p. 44).

Through control of genetic processes, we will gain greater freedom over nature, but it is altogether possible that human freedom will negate human dignity. The report notes the possible use of amniocentesis to predict the sex of a fetus and to abort until parental choice is satisfied. The enhanced freedom of the parents would mean an assault on the dignity of the unwanted gender (most likely female) and therefore on the dignity of the human species as a whole.

In 1983 the National Council of Churches Panel on Bioethical Concerns produced a report that was published with additional materials as *Genetic Engineering: Social and Ethical Consequences* (National Council of Churches 1984). This report is less precisely written than the 1980 statement, yet it opens new possibilities for theological assessment of genetic engineering.

The report speaks of the new genetic technology as a gift given to human society by its developers. It understands the gift within the context of God's continuous creativity. Through the manipulation of the molecular basis of organisms, scientists are opening new arenas in which divine creativity might have free play. In pursuing this technology, we should recognize that we are dealing with transcending values of creativity and life; "such technology is never just the joining of 'mere bits of matter' " (National Council of Churches 1984, p. 23).

As human beings, we are part of creation and must live within the limits of our place. Yet of all creatures, we are exalted with the identity of being in the divine image and having dominion—which the report understands as stewardship and responsibility—over the rest of the creation. Being in God's image, human beings are creative in ways that reflect God's creativity, and we should use our creative powers to extend God's. "Therefore, we are called to live in harmony with all of creation, including humankind, and to participate with the Creator in the fulfillment of creation." New technologies open the possibility that human beings are able to exercise a beneficial "dominion" over the creation and "that men and women are coming into the full exercise of their given powers of co-creation" (National Council of Churches 1984, pp. 24–25).

After suggesting the image of "co-creation," the report declines to go further and suggest what it means or what its limits might be. It observes that "the language of co-creation must be used with care, however" (National Council of Churches 1984, p. 24). But it does not say why care should be used or what conditions should be attached to the term.

Unfortunately, this kind of ambivalence characterizes the whole report. For example, in spite of a generally positive stance toward the new technology, the report anticipates horrible outcomes, but then only calls for caution: "When the subject is recombinant DNA, when the concern is the total gene pool for humankind, when the scenario is extinction of species or eugenic programs, or when the whole biosphere can be affected by any one experiment with new life forms *ad nova*, extreme caution can be our legitimate response" (National Council of the Churches of Christ 1984, p. 30). The first clauses are wildly overstated, but if they are thought to refer to real possibilities, then the final clause is pitifully weak.

In May 1986 the Governing Board of the National Council of Churches adopted a statement titled "Genetic Science for Human Benefit." The report surveys developments and applications of genetic engineering and its impact on human beings. Reflecting on theological themes in reference to genetic engineering, the report affirms the value of each human life in relation to God, not in relation to some human standard of health. While the pursuit of health is good, the report cautions that the ultimate meaning of our lives "is a goal offered in Christ by faith, not a promised possibility of human achievement." In this context, the report does not rule out entirely the possibility of human germline research: "Gene therapy of germ-line, or sex, cells of human embryos—if ever practicable—will deserve especially stringent control" (National Council of Churches 1986, p. 13).

Two questions of justice are identified. First, will the poor, especially in developing countries, have equal access to the benefits of this technology? Will they and their environments be exploited for purposes of experimentation? Second, will there be "monopolistic ownership of genetically modified organisms or substances which are known to be essential to human life for nourishment and health?" These questions are not answered, but they indicate the concerns of the authors.

The report notes that much of the research upon which commercial applications of genetic engineering are based was originally funded by government monies. It asks, "Should the government lay claim to a portion of individual or corporate profits? Or, at least, insist on satisfactory contributions to public health and well being?" (National Council of Churches 1986, p. 10). The report affirms "that companies and legislators should devise ways for the public at large to share in the benefits or profits made on the sale of products, the basic development of which has been enabled by public funding for research" (National Council of Churches 1986, p. 14).

The report goes on to call for a public commission on genetic engineering. "The commission should possess sufficient powers to exercise reasonable public review and to establish guidelines as required by the public interest" (National Council of Churches 1986, p. 15).

The statement concludes by asking what role churches should play in the future development of genetic engineering. Several points are noted. First, the churches can play a significant role in contributing to public understanding of genetic engineering. Second, churches and their agencies should support "research and education on the scientific, sociological and political aspects of [biotechnology], as well as on the theological, ethical and moral ones." Third, "Theological seminaries in particular should provide basic education in genetic counseling and its pastoral implication." And fourth, those with "advanced theological knowledge should be challenged and encouraged to become involved in the urgent study and discussion of genetic issues" (National Council of Churches 1986, p. 16).

Other Ecumenical Positions

In 1983 a wide-ranging group of sixty-four United States clergy signed a resolution calling for a halt to attempts to alter the human germline. The heads of many United States denominations, several Catholic bishops, and Jewish leaders endorsed a statement written by anti–genetic engineering activist Jeremy Rifkin. After a series of clauses, the resolution itself simply asserts "that efforts to engineer specific genetic traits into the germline of the human species should not be attempted" (Foundation on Economic Trends 1983).

The event provoked considerable reaction in the scientific and popular press, which apparently was the intent of most of the signatories. While Rifkin himself believes that no human germline research should ever be done, some who signed were not so adamant. A number who signed "said that they are not yet sure they want a total ban, but signed the resolution to stimulate a broad public debate on the issues" (Norman 1983, p. 1360). In fact, it is important to recall that the 1986 statement of the National Council of Churches, whose member churches include many of the denominations whose heads signed Rifkin's resolution, specifically leaves the door open to human germline research. Finally, a question of misrepresentation is raised by the resolution: It calls for a halt to something (namely, germline research) that is not occurring; in so doing the resolution implies that scientists are guilty of engaging in this line of research.

A few weeks after the Rifkin resolution was signed, a group of religious scholars and scientists met to discuss genetic engineering. Under the sponsorship of the Institute on Religion in an Age of Science, the conference drafted a statement of prospects and recommendations. Among the recommendations was an endorsement of somatic cell gene therapy, but the statement was also concerned that "germ line intervention should be approached with extreme care because of the possible risks to future persons" (Davis and Engelhardt 1984, p. 280). In addition, the report urged the establishment of a continuing commission, diverse in membership, to "review the moral and public policy issues raised by future advances, or likely advances, in molecular genetics and gene therapy" (Davis and Engelhardt 1984, p. 280).

Protestant Denominations in the United States

Only a few United States Protestant denominations have offered statements on genetic engineering. For example, in 1985 the General Convention of the Episcopal Church passed a brief resolution that "encourages genetic engineering research to increase human understanding of vital processes" (Episcopal Church 1985). The resolution continues with an endorsement of pharmaceutical uses of genetic engineering and appeals to those responsible for theological education to provide seminary and continuing education in genetics, particularly in support of the clergy role in genetic counseling.

A 1989 pronouncement by the General Synod of the United Church of Christ recognizes scientific research as a Christian calling through which the believer imitates the feeding and healing ministry of Jesus of Nazareth. In generally positive tones, the statement urges public discussion of emerging applications. "Genetic engineering opens new ways for people of

compassion to help those in need. With caution and yet with great hopeful-
ness, we welcome its development, pledging to support a climate of
thoughtful reflection, public awareness, appropriate regulation and justice
in distribution" (United Church of Christ 1989). Concern for the economic
impact of genetic engineering is noted, as is concern for genetic diversity.
In addition, the pronouncement calls for corporations to set research priorities by humanitarian and not strictly market considerations.

In 1992 the United Methodist Church approved the adoption of a
major report on genetics. In its draft version, the report recognizes the
broad theological significance of genetics and genetic engineering
(United Methodist Church 1991, p. 18). Technology, including genetic
engineering, opens new avenues for our responsible stewardship of
creation. "Humans are to participate in, manage, nurture, justly
distribute, employ, develop and enhance creation's resources in accor-
dance with God's revealed purposes" (United Methodist Church 1991,
p. 18). Since we are created in the image of God, our role in nature is
sharply defined by our creaturely status.

The report makes reference to the redemptive as well as to the
creative work of God. The link between redemption and genetics,
however, is limited to the acceptance of genetic diversity:

> Through the saving work of Christ, God has claimed all persons as
> beloved sons and daughters with inherent worth and dignity. Therefore,
> we understand that our worth as children of God is irrespective of genetic
> qualities, personal attributes or achievements. Barriers and prejudices
> based on biological characteristics fracture the human family and distort
> God's goal for humanity. Unity based upon the divinely given worth of all
> persons characterizes the community of all persons within which the
> community of Christ bears witness to this truth. Such unity respects and
> embraces genetic diversity which accounts for many differences among
> people. (United Methodist Church 1991, p. 19)

In clear language, the report anticipates that genetics research will indicate that some differences between individuals are explained genetically.
More important, the report urges that the Christian community accept all
persons fully and equally, regardless of genetic variance.

Addressing the institutions of the United Methodist Church, the
report calls for increased education of "laity and clergy on the issues of
genetic science, theology, and ethics" (United Methodist Church 1991, p.
19). Local churches and judicatories are urged "to become centers for
dialogue," and the report requests that clergy "be trained to provide
pastoral counseling for persons with genetic disorders and their families
as well as those facing difficult choices as a result of genetic testing"
(United Methodist Church 1991, p. 19). In addition, the report urges theological seminaries to "equip clergy to deal theologically and ethically
with science and technology" (United Methodist Church 1991, p. 19).

Roman Catholic Positions

Roman Catholic statements on genetic engineering, both from the United States and from the Vatican, look favorably on genetic engineering, in spite of deep-seated Catholic opposition to various forms of birth technology. As early as 1977 the Committee for Human Values of the United States Catholic Conference prepared a statement for presentation to the United States bishops. The report calls for extensive discussion, inside the church and beyond. Because of the pace of research, this discussion is urgent. However,

> that urgency should not be allowed to short circuit reflection on: the purpose and implications of these forms of DNA modification; the effect of this type of genetic research on our understanding of ourselves and of our relation to nature; and the correlation between the scientific advance possible through recombinant DNA research and human progress as judged by a variety of criteria. (United States Catholic Conference 1977, p. 772)

Public discussion between scientists and the general public "is necessary if wisdom and humility are to effect enlightened public policy" (United States Catholic Conference 1977, p. 772).

In 1982 Pope John Paul II addressed a group of researchers who had assembled for a week of study on the social implications of their work. While he condemned experiments that involved human embryos, the Pope endorsed research involving animals, since they "are at the service of man and can hence be the object of experimentation" (John Paul II 1982, p. 342). The Pope offered approval of research toward somatic cell therapy to treat such diseases as sickle cell anemia, even if this therapy is performed in utero (John Paul II 1982, p. 343).

This view was reiterated in 1983 in an address by John Paul II to a group of physicians. While accepting somatic gene therapy, the Pope warned that "the biological nature of every human is untouchable (John Paul II 1983, p. 388). There is some ambiguity of meaning in the term "genetic manipulation," the Pope observes, that needs to be removed by careful discussion. Because of this ambiguity, he prefers the term "genetic surgery," since it connotes a correction rather than an enhancement of nature. "Some are beginning to talk of 'genetic surgery,' so as to show better that the physician intervenes, not in order to modify nature, but to help it develop along its line, that of creation, that willed by God. In working in this obviously delicate domain, the researcher follows God's design" (John Paul II 1983, p. 389).

Because of consistent opposition to abortion, recent Catholic teaching is cautious in dealing with prenatal genetic screening. Screening that is therapeutic in intent is permissible. But genetic screening "is gravely opposed to the moral law when it is done with the thought of possibly inducing an abortion depending upon the results: A diagnosis which shows the existence of a malformation or a hereditary illness must not be the equivalent of a death sentence" (John Paul II 1987, p. 702).

Conclusions

Despite the fact that the perspectives we have reviewed in this chapter sometimes conflict with one another, especially when they touch on reproductive technologies, it is possible nonetheless to describe several major themes that are widely shared among them. For example, it is affirmed that human beings are created in the image of God. This dignifies the human role in nature but imposes two limits on that role. First, God is God, and we human beings are not to act in any way that contradicts the purposes of God as we have come to know them through the texts of the Christian tradition. Second, we are to remember that we are creatures, not metaphysically distinct from all else that God has created but interdependent participants in an ongoing creative process. We human beings are part of nature. We are not supernatural aliens passing through nature to a destiny beyond nature, nor is nature our foe.

These statements also emphasize that cultural or social values will shape the development and use of genetics. By influencing this social context, the churches may influence the future development and use of the technology. Concern is expressed that the benefits of technology be widely distributed and that the risks be fairly shared. Some of the writers believe that our sinful human nature will prevent us from fully seeing the misuses of our technology.

Another concern raised in several documents is that genetics research and genetic engineering will reinforce reductionist ideas about living systems or organisms and about human personhood. This tendency is lamented but not effectively countered in the documents we have considered.

The documents generally take an ambiguous view of the moral condition of nature. On the one hand, all the writers agree that persons with illnesses, including genetic disorders, are to be treated, their symptoms relieved, and, if possible, their illnesses cured. But the documents are silent on the underlying philosophical question: Is illness natural or a defect of nature? They are equally silent on the corresponding theological question: Does God will illness or its cure? Their reticence may arise from this dilemma: On the one hand, these writers want to affirm the full humanity of persons with genetic diseases, while, on the other hand, they want to affirm the legitimacy of preventing or treating genetic disorders.

The statements readily speak of genetic engineering in relation to the doctrine of creation but rarely in relation to redemption. Similarly, God's relationship with nature is pictured as that of Creator but not as Redeemer. God is seen as endlessly embellishing the creation but not restoring it or reordering it. Here again, the moral relationship between God and disease (or any kind of natural disorder) is unclear in these documents. As a result, human participation with God is limited to "co-creation." We are permitted to explore novel genetic combinations with God. But are we also permitted to identify and correct genetic defects? Is God redeeming nature, and are we called to participate technologically in this work of redemption?

5

Redemption and Technology

For all their differences, the four Gospels agree in identifying Jesus of Nazareth as a healer of the sick. In story after story, Jesus is portrayed as a compassionate healer. Yet is it precisely on this most obvious and unanimous point that modern theology has experienced great difficulty. Miracles are widely seen as impossible since they are thought to violate the laws of nature as understood by science. Since miraculous healings are impossible, modern theology largely agrees that they could not have happened as the Gospels claim.

As a result of this view of miracles, a wedge is driven between Jesus and the healings. Since he could not have done them, the reports are seen as theologically irrelevant to his identity. So the Jesus Christ of modern theology is distanced from the healings, from the human body, and from nature itself. And since the redemptive work of God is centered in Christ, nature falls outside the sphere of both Christ and redemption. As a result, Christ and redemption are limited in scope to human consciousness, which is often regarded as nonnatural.

Because of this distance between nature and Christ, nature is most often approached theologically without reference to Christ and redemption. When that occurs, nature is seen only as that which God is *creating*, while the redemption and transformation of nature are overlooked. This chapter will argue that it is more appropriate to view nature as that which God is *creating and redeeming*. Not only is that more appropriate in respect to the Gospel accounts and the Christian tradition; it is also a more adequate framework within which to understand genetic engineering.

We have asked about the purpose of genetic engineering, noting the problems that arise when we try to say that the purpose of genetic engineering is to benefit humanity or to benefit nature. We have argued that some of these problems are removed when we maintain that the purpose of genetic engineering is to serve and glorify God. But how do we know God's purposes for nature? How do we have confidence that we can serve God's purposes through technology? These are the questions to which we now turn. First, we will argue that the creative and redemptive purposes of God are disclosed in the relationship between Jesus Christ and nature. Then we will discuss the traditional view that nature is good yet disordered as a result of the fall. Next, we will ask whether it is possible to understand the goodness and the disorder of nature in evolutionary terms, without a historic fall. Then we will review the position of traditional writers who saw technology as our participation in God's redemptive work. Finally, we will ask how far it is possible to see genetic engineering as our own involvement in God's redemption of nature.

Christ and the Redemption of Nature

The Christian idea of God originates with the stories of Jesus of Nazareth, whom Christians believe to be the definitive expression of God's character and purpose. While each New Testament Gospel offers a distinct portrait of the life of Jesus and a distinct theological interpretation of that life, they agree in this: Jesus of Nazareth devoted a major share of his attention and energy to the healing of the sick. Stories about healings are central to the identity of Jesus in the Gospels (Matthew 11:2–6). "Healing in the gospels and elsewhere in the New Testament is a central factor in primitive Christianity, and was so from the beginning of the movement" (Kee 1986, p. 124). The Gospel writers note that they see Jesus' healings as motivated by pity or compassion (cf. Matthew 20:34). These healings were not merely a way of calling attention to a more important teaching mission. They are presented as essential to the identity of Jesus, who in turn is taken to be the definitive expression of the character of the divine.

Over the past two hundred years, theological scholarship has asked the critical question, to what extent should stories of healings be regarded as historic reports? Our concern here is to go beyond the critical question and to inquire into the meaning of the confession, made by each of the Gospels, as to the identity of Jesus Christ and his relationship with nature. Rather than ask the critical question about the historical accuracy of these stories, we want to ask about the view of the relationship between God and nature that the stories presuppose.

When the stories claim that Jesus healed, was he seen as thwarting the will of God the Creator? Or is Jesus seen as acting on behalf of God and as an expression of God's intentions? If Jesus is seen as thwarting the will of God the Creator, then his whole identity as a revelation of the divine is called into question. Jesus would then become a Promethean rebel against the tyranny of the gods or a demon in league with Satan. He is rebuked by his critics on this very point. His answer, of course, is that he resists evil through the power of God (Matthew 12:22–32). The actions of Jesus are seen by his followers as completely consistent with the purposes of God.

There are at least three reasons why we can be quite certain that Jesus' contemporaries saw his ability to heal as a manifestation of God's power and will. First, the God of Judaism was confessed to be *a healing God* (Kee

1986, pp. 12–16). "I am the Lord, your healer," Exodus 15:26b (RSV) announces. "I kill and I make alive; I wound and I heal," Deuteronomy 32:39a (RSV) warns. Howard Clark Kee notes that Israel saw Yahweh as one who heals through the gift of personal salvation and the restoration of moral wholeness. Furthermore, Israel's understanding of God as healer includes the healing or restoration of nature, such as the transformation of the Salt Sea into a freshwater lake (Kee 1986, pp. 14–15). In Isaiah 51, for example, we read of a redemptive *reversal toward Eden*:

> For the Lord will comfort Zion;
>   he will comfort all her waste places,
> and will make her wilderness like Eden,
>   her desert like the garden of the Lord
>   (Isaiah 51:3, RSV)

Eden here becomes the symbol of the end or goal of God's work.

A second reason why Jesus' followers saw his healing power as a manifestation of God was this: In the Jewish apocalyptic world view of that time, sickness was taken to be the work of demons. Demons, understood to be fallen angels let loose in the world, pervert God's creation. Since sickness had a spiritual cause, only a greater spiritual power could reverse it. Jesus' healings are pictured as direct spiritual rebukes of demons, in some cases involving exorcism (Kee 1986, p. 73). Since God alone possessed this power, Jesus was seen as a manifestation of the power of God.

The third reason that the healings of Jesus were seen as manifestations of divine power lies in the link between physical healing and the forgiveness of sins. According to the theology of Jesus' followers, only God could forgive sins. Yet Jesus often announced the forgiveness of sins as a preparation for physical healing, thereby linking the healing with the activity of God.

For these three reasons, it appears certain that the healing activities of Jesus are taken by his contemporaries to be a manifestation of the power of God and therefore compatible with the intentions of God. Jesus' actions are manifestations or expressions in narrative form of what God intends for the creation, particularly in respect to the health of human beings.

The stories of Jesus as a healer are accompanied by sayings, attributed to Jesus, about nature. Frequently in these sayings, Jesus uses agricultural and biological examples or parables of the reign of God. He describes God's influence in the world by pointing to the planting of seeds, to the mixture of wheat and weeds, to the growth of yeast, or to a shepherd's search for a lost lamb. He encourages his listeners to trust God's providential care. After all, the lilies of the field do not make their clothes, but they are more magnificently dressed than King Solomon. God, who notices when a sparrow falls, knows our needs.

Interestingly, early in the Gospel accounts, Jesus himself is tempted three times by Satan to misuse his divine powers and to cooperate with rebellion against God. According to Matthew's version, Jesus is first enticed to command stones to become bread. In the view of the Gospel writers, there is no doubt that Jesus could have done this, or that he was hungry, or that it was morally appropriate for him to be fed. Jesus rejects the suggestion, however, and considers it a temptation (Matthew 4:1–4). It is probably safe to say that in rejecting the suggestion, Jesus is not rejecting the act of making bread and feeding himself, but rejecting the use of his power to satisfy his own needs or to attain his own ends. The Gospels present him as using his power out of compassion for others and not as a means of self-advancement or self-preservation. In the third temptation, Jesus is offered control over the nations if he will worship Satan and join the revolt against God. Jesus rejects this with the assertion that God only is to be served (Matthew 4:8–10).

With their stories of healings and with their sayings of Jesus, the Gospels portray Jesus as one who delighted in nature and yet who altered it again and again in order to restore it. On the one hand, Jesus affirms the goodness of nature, accepts it with gratitude, and trusts it because it enjoys the providential care of a faithful God. But on the other hand, nature is also experienced as disease or as untimely death. For Jesus and for the first Christians, disease and death were not seen as part of God's intentions. Quite the contrary—God was seen as opposed to them. Nature could be seen as simultaneously good and flawed because of the belief that disease was attributable to demons and other rebellious forces, including sinful human beings. Over these forces God has ultimate but not immediate control, and so they are temporarily free to act in ways that are contrary to God's good intentions.

Beyond the Gospels, other New Testament writers proclaim Jesus as the healer of creation. Creation is fundamentally good and affirmed as such, but it can go awry and be corrupted by the power of demons or evil spirits. In acting to correct this damage through the healing of the sick, Jesus heals the creation where it is corrupted. Paul, for example, portrays Jesus Christ as the conqueror of the creation's great enemy, death (1 Corinthians 15). Death is seen by Paul as a perversion of God's original creation, occasioned by human sin. By overcoming sin, Jesus Christ eventually destroys death.

Elsewhere in the New Testament (cf. John 1:1–14 or Colossians 1:15–17), Jesus Christ is proclaimed as both Creator and Redeemer. Christian scriptures thus preserve the Hebrew belief in the original goodness of the creation, joining it with the later notion of apocalyptic Judaism that nature needs redemption. Jesus Christ does not come to repair the inferior work of a lesser god, nor is he a demiurge coaxing matter to submit to form, as Plato portrays creation in the *Timaeus*. Christ comes to reclaim his own creation from the effects of creaturely sin and rebellion. Christianity is thus creation-affirming *and* creation-transforming. Rudolf Bultmann (1951, 1955) notes this twofold view of nature: "The creation has a peculiarly ambiguous character: on the one hand, it is the earth placed by God at man's disposal for his use and benefit (1 Cor. 10:26) . . . ; on the other, it is the field of activity for evil, demonic powers" (1951, p. 230).

Aspects of the present created order are contrary to the will of the Creator, but creation as a whole remains valuable and worth redeeming. The goal of salvation is not to escape creation or to seek its destruction but to transform it and to free it from corrupting powers. At the core of the Christian view is the recognition that nature is good yet flawed. This view of nature is basic to the portrayal of Jesus found in the Gospels and in early Christian proclamation. There can be no doubt that the Gospels portray Jesus as one who affirmed the goodness of nature as God's creation. But the accounts of the healings demonstrate that Jesus was also seen as acting to correct and restore a disordered nature.

Curse
Gen.

The Source of Disorder

To account for the goodness *and* the disorder of nature, traditional Christianity affirmed that God is the creator of nature and the guarantor of its worth, but that rebellious angels and fallen human beings account for a world-pervading disorder. The drama of redemption lies in undoing the damage of this disorder and in freeing the creation for the consummation of God's intentions. It is important to distinguish between the *core affirmation* that nature is good yet disordered and its *explanation,* namely, that the disorder is the result of the fall. The core affirmation should be preserved by contemporary Christian theology. It is basic to the view of technology and genetic engineering developed here. The *explanation* of disorder as the result of a fall of angels and of the first human beings, however, is not needed by contemporary Christian theology or for our argument. I have no interest in defending this explanation, even though I wish to preserve the core affirmation that nature is good but disordered. In order to preserve it, I will suggest an alternative explanation of creation's disorder. Before I do so, however, let us review the traditional explanation, noting especially the place of technology within that explanation.

The traditional explanation of nature's disorder asserts that sin, angelic and human, is the cause of the disarray. Sin is not something God creates, although God creates the condition that makes sin possible, namely, the existence of free agents. Through the choice of angels and human beings, sin enters the creation, disturbs its harmony and beauty, and affects all other species by making them violent and disorderly. John Hick summarizes this conviction:

> That the animal species prey upon on another, that there are microbes and
> bacteria which cause disease in animal bodies, that there are weaknesses

in the earth's crust producing volcanoes and tornadoes, that there are violent extremes of temperature, uninhabitable climates, droughts and blights, may all be due to the malevolence or heedlessness of higher beings who were appointed as nature's guardians but who have become enemies of nature's God. (Hick 1966, p. 367)

In the mid-1700s the English reformer John Wesley wrote, "It is an evident truth, that the whole animate creation is punished for Adam's sin" (1978 [1756], p. 319).

The earth is not exactly what God intends it to be, nor is it the home God intends for human beings. The sin of Adam and Eve affects nature, and nature turns on humanity in revenge: "The heavens, the earth, and all things contained therein, conspire to punish the rebels against their Creator. The sun and moon shed unwholsome influences from above; the earth exhales poisonous damps from beneath; the beasts of the field, the birds of the air, the fishes of the sea, are in a state of hostility" (John Wesley 1973 [1755], pp. 9–10). Human beings were created to be at home on earth and to have dominion over the other creatures except angels. Before the fall, agriculture and childbirth were to be part of human existence, but they were to be pursued and enjoyed under the conditions of order. By their disobedience, Adam and Eve seek disorder in their own relationship with God. God punishes them with disorder in their relationship with nature. "In the punishment of that sin the retribution for disobedience is simply disobedience itself" (Augustine 1984 [*City of God* XIV 15], p. 575). God makes nature disobedient to Adam and Eve, so that agriculture, childbirth, and all other relations with nature become frighteningly unpredictable and dangerous.

Since we are part of nature, our own nature is affected, almost as a genetic defect: "The seeds of wickedness and pain, of sickness and death, are now lodged in our inmost substance; whence a thousand disorders continually spring, even without the aid of external violence" (John Wesley 1973 [1755], p. 9). This not only causes us to be sick but also means that our whole being is disordered. Our intellect and our will are affected, so that they lack their original integrity.

As recently as a century ago, theologians argued that the fall brought about something like a genetic defect that all human beings inherit through biological propagation (Smith 1955). Horace Bushnell, whose views on religious education became widely influential, argued that human beings inherit the disorder of their parents through a line of biological descent. Drawing upon the prevailing view that acquired traits are inherited (a view often associated with Lamarck), Bushnell argued that the misdeeds of all our ancestors are inherited biologically as predispositions to the same misbehavior. Since good behavior is also inheritable, religious education makes a difference not only for the generation that is being educated but also for their offspring (Bushnell

1903 [1888]). Twenty years later, when Lamarckianism was being increasingly rejected by scientific authorities, F. R. Tennant (1902) argued that Adam and Eve could not *acquire* a trait that could then be propagated through biological descent. Tennant agreed, however, that human beings inherit inclinations that are morally disordered and sought to argue his view on the basis of newly emerging Darwinian thought (Tennant 1902). During the years immediately after Tennant, several other theologians took up the challenge of reformulating the notion of inheritable human disorder in evolutionary terms. In the next section, we will ask whether Tennant's program should be taken up again.

Disorder Without a Fall

The traditional explanation of the sources of disorder, of course, is no longer convincing to many people. Even before the Darwinian assault on Adam and Eve, the idea of a historic fall as an explanation of disorder was widely rejected among theologians (Smith 1955). The improbability of a historic fall within an evolutionary framework only completed what had begun centuries earlier: The fall could no longer account for nature's disorder. Christian theology (with the exception of Tennant and a few others) proceeded to reinterpret traditional ideas about the fall and redemption in psychological and relational motifs of guilt and reconciliation. In doing so, many theologians over the past century have isolated human sin as the sole problem in creation. Of course, human sin is a serious problem in creation, for it breeds not only violence and injustice but also environmental exploitation. Seen in this light, technology is an expansion of sin, since it distorts an otherwise innocent creation. By contrast, I want to argue that in addition to human sin, and even prior to human sin, <u>creation is good yet disordered</u>, and thus that technology has a role to play in serving the order God intends. Furthermore, the disorder of nature permeates human nature, disordering the human person from the beginning.

If the core conviction that nature is <u>good yet flawed</u> cannot be supported by the traditional explanation of the fall, may it be supported some other way? Since the writings of Thomas Huxley a century ago (1947 [1893]), with which Tennant was familiar, scientific writers have suggested that Darwin's theory of evolution leads to an outlook on nature that values natural processes as the source of creativity, yet recognizes the moral ambiguity of the processes and their outcomes. More recently, Wilson (1975), Dawkins (1976), and Alexander (1987) have continued this interpretation of Darwinian theory.

At the same time, empirical research in behavioral genetics promises to clarify the interplay between genes, environment, and personal responsibility. This research attempts to find correlations between variations in all our behavioral tendencies, good and bad, and our genetic inheritance. As research clarifies the role of genes in behavior, theology will be pressed to clarify the role, if any, of personal responsibility and of divine grace. If genetics research succeeded in convincing people that their beliefs and behaviors are *nothing but the effect of their genes*, theology would be seriously threatened. Theologians, drawing upon genetics research itself, need to argue against this possible confusion in the popular interpretation of behavioral genetics.

Fortunately for theology, the strongest support for a continuing emphasis on personal responsibility comes from behavioral genetics research itself. Current research suggests that while variations in certain behaviors and attitudes depend upon our genes, the dependence is only about 50 percent, meaning that other factors are as important as our genetic inheritance in accounting for behavioral variations among individuals. Often, when people hear that some trait or feature has a genetic explanation, they think that it is genetically *determined*. This is based on a misunderstanding of the interplay between genes and the environment. Furthermore, when we are discussing the genetic basis for behavior, we are typically considering traits or patterns toward which many genes *contribute*. It is not likely that any single gene by itself causes a behavioral trait (Plomin 1990). The combined effects of many genes are required, and this combined effect is further influenced (at about 50 percent) by the environment. Behavioral genetics research will yield greater precision on the environment, since some of the studies compare twins and siblings reared together with those reared apart.

In developing a theological understanding of the interplay between genes and environment, theologians should avoid thinking that there is no genetic basis for behavior or personality type. It is equally mistaken, however, to think that if there is a genetic basis to behavior, then behavior is genetically *determined*. Furthermore, it is dubious metaphysics to try to avoid these first two mistakes by assuming that in addition to the genetically conditioned organism, there is an essential self or soul that is immune from genetic factors and that can therefore be considered without regard to genetics. While many traditional Christian theologians made this dualistic assumption, it is questionable whether the Hebrew and Christian scriptures did.

Christian thinkers who are able to appropriate the insight emerging from genetics research are now acquiring what Augustine and other traditional theologians lacked, namely, an empirical basis for understanding the heritability of human disorder. Genetics research indicates that we all inherit genetic defects that affect our physical and personal qualities. In a very general way, this supports the traditional theological notion of the disordered self. But with this general support, genetics challenges the traditional theological notion in three respects, each of which should be the subject for future theological research.

First, where traditional views of fallenness claimed that we were created innocent and then fell into disorder, genetics research, together with the theory of evolution, suggests that genetic inclinations for good and evil are acquired through the same process of genetic inheritance. Aggression and altruism evolve together. The relationship between aggression and altruism is intricate and not yet well understood, according to Carolyn Zahn-Waxler, E. Cummings, and Ronald Iannotti (1986). Richard Alexander (1987) attempts to understand altruism as a modification of genetic selfishness. By becoming increasingly cooperative within groups, human beings and their biological ancestors increased their chances of reproduction (Alexander 1987). Future research should clarify further the origin and the heritability of aggression and altruism.

Second, genetics research will inevitably reveal the extent to which human selves are shaped by genes. In the past, theologians often thought of selves or souls as inhabiting bodies but as largely unaffected by anything bodily. This view, of course, depended upon a psychological dualism of soul and body, a dualism not characteristic of scriptural texts and one that is generally avoided by contemporary thinkers. If this dualism is avoided, and if, in its place, we think of the self or the soul as the coherence within the complexity of the human organism, then this coherence of the self is genetically conditioned through and through. There is no nongenetic or nonorganic soul, subsisting in an ethereal or spiritual substance. The soul subsists in the brain, and in whatever way our genes have structured our brain, they have also given us the substratum of our soul. When the sense of self emerges as coherent consciousness, it attains a freedom to interact, as an irreducibly psychological phenomenon, with the biological. But that freedom is itself given in our genes and limited by them. We are on our way toward understanding the relationship between genes, proteins, brain cells, and the entire central nervous system. As we attain a detailed understanding of ourselves, from our genes to our brains, theology will need to absorb this insight and to maintain a view of the human that preserves a sense of the wonder of the human self without resorting to dualism.

Third, genetic research will begin to show us how much we human beings differ genetically from one another. We already know that each individual carries a unique combination of genes and that these genes contribute to our individually distinctive appearance. As we unravel the relationship between genes and behavior, we will also learn that we have each inherited a unique genetic behavioral makeup. Traditionally, theology and philosophy assumed that each human self or soul is virtually equal in spiritual capacity and in moral predisposition. Since the self or the soul was unaffected by such things as genetic inheritance, differences in individuals' genes made no difference in their souls. But now we are learning that our personhood is conditioned by our genetic inheritance, and since our genes are individually unique, we are unique persons, each varying at the core of our self from every other person. Part of the variance, of course, is due to our unique personal history retained in our memory. But another important part of our individuality, as we are now discovering, is due to the uniqueness of our genes.

In the future Christian theology will have to be more aware of individual variation between human persons. Our capacity for the moral and spiritual life is a genetically conditioned one, and therefore it is a capacity that we inherit in varying ways and degrees. Indeed, since the moral and spiritual life consists of a wide range of behaviors, traits, and habits of mind and heart, each of which is genetically conditioned, we therefore inherit a spiritual and moral inclination that is individually unique. Our inclinations to selfishness and sin are also uniquely our own. This means that our spiritual struggles are unique. What tempts one may not interest another. What comes easily to one might be unattainable to another. We are different at our core—in our DNA—and theology in the future will have to recognize these differences. Research into faith and moral development, for example, will need to be done by first taking into account individual genetic variation. Even more important, the Christian message of grace and salvation will need to be individually contoured.

Whether the traditional doctrine of the fall can and should be reinterpreted once again in light of evolutionary science and behavioral genetics remains one of the great questions faced by contemporary theology. Such a reinterpretation has no stake in defending an outdated view of natural history or a demonology. What it would seek to articulate and to clarify are the convictions that nature is good but morally disordered, that good and disorder are pervasive and inevitable by-products of the evolutionary process, that a predisposition toward good and evil is genetically inheritable, and that good and disorder affect human intellect and will. Such a reinterpretation would identify the source of disorder within the physical stuff of the creation. The disorder would not be seen as arising from the pride or selfishness of will, seen traditionally as residing in the nonmaterial soul. Nor would it spring from a single act of of disobedience, either of Satan or of Adam and Eve. Rather, both the good and the disorder would be seen as the cumulative by-product of countless events in the evolutionary history of life on earth. We human beings, arriving late in that history, inherit this history in our genes. It affects our intellects and wills just as it affects our morphology. Human intellect and will are not nonmaterial but arise through the complexity of the human brain, an evolved organ. Culture, which includes science, technology, and religion, arises from the evolved capacity of human beings to communicate and to comprehend. Along with religion and morality, science and technology are grounded in the evolved capacities of the brain. All these cultural phenomena are conditioned by the evolutionary history accumulated in our genes.

Whatever disorder accompanies evolution will affect our intellect and our will, our faith and our technology.

Failure to view nature as good but morally disordered will have three consequences that bear directly upon our understanding of a technology such as genetic engineering. First, if we were to take the view that nature is *only disordered*, we would act as if its value lay strictly in its usefulness to us. Nature would be seen as worthless raw materials waiting to be manufactured to the specifications of our desires. We would fail to see that nature has aesthetic and moral values in reference to its Creator, and that we must respect and preserve these values. Unfortunately, our modern approach toward nature seems shaped by this conviction. Christian theology can play a helpful role in asserting the goodness of nature in reference to God the Creator.

Second, without the conviction that nature is good but disordered and that *we inherit its disorder*, we will have too optimistic a regard of our own moral capabilities. We are profoundly implicated in the moral disorder of nature, and our own capacities for ethical reasoning are evolved through the same processes that account for the goodness and the disorder of all living things. These ethical capacities, which guide our understanding of technology and of the appropriateness of its development and use, are affected by the disorders that our technology seeks to correct. How can we have any confidence that we will use our powers to correct disorder rather than to increase and extend it? How can technology accomplish anything for us other than the extension of our selfishness and shortsightedness? We can only presume to redeem nature if we recognize that we ourselves are in need of redemption.

Third, without the conviction that nature is good *but also disordered*, it will be difficult for us to say what we are attempting to accomplish with our technology. It is, after all, disorder and its effects that we are trying to correct. The very notion of a defective gene, for example, requires such a conviction if it is to an be intelligible concept. A gene is identified for research and possible therapy because it causes human suffering. But it is regarded as a genetic defect because it is taken as a manifestation of the moral disorder of nature in reference to the intentions of the Creator for the creation, for the human species, and for the individuals affected by the genetic abnormality.

James Gustafson (1981, 1984) argues helpfully that there is a discernible order in nature that lays a moral claim upon us and to which we must consent. "The vocation of the human community is to consent to the divine governance, to cooperate with it (not merely be resigned to it) toward those aims that can be discerned" (Gustafson 1981, p. 242). The divine governance of the world, for Gustafson, lies in the ordering of nature that is disclosed through the study of nature.

What is missing in Gustafson's argument is a recognition of disorder in nature. Gustafson notes that technology uses the order of nature to alter nature: "While we can, in modern cultures, intervene in these processes to alter them, we still consent to them in a significant measure, cooperating with them as they are given. If a chromosomal defect cannot be corrected, we can consent to it (not merely resign ourselves to it) and participate in the development of a limited natural capacity" (Gustafson 1981, p. 241). On what grounds may we regard a "chromosomal defect" as a *defect?* It has arisen through the ordering processes of nature, which Gustafson takes as a manifestation of the divine to which the appropriate moral response is consent. By linking God and nature so closely and by ignoring the theological significance of the relationship between God and nature disclosed in Jesus of Nazareth, Gustafson offers no conceptual framework in which we may think about a *defect of nature*. Since God and nature are so strongly linked, it is hard to see that any aspect of nature could be regarded as contrary to God's intentions. Yet this is precisely what we must be able to conceive if we are to come to a theological understanding of genetic engineering. What is a genetic defect? Can a genetic condition be regarded theologically as defective— that is, defective in reference to God?

By approaching the question from the starting point of the relationship between Jesus and nature, we have the necessary framework for comprehending the notion of a genetic defect. A human genetic defect is that which causes a condition comparable to those which evoked the compassionate intervention of Jesus of Nazareth and which is therefore disclosed as contrary to the purposes of God. The very notion of "genetic defect," central to the emerging field of human genetic medicine, is a hybrid notion involving both scientific and theological dimensions. The science of genetics, of course, must locate and describe the specific genetic anomaly that gives rise to a recognizable human condition. But it is culture that labels the condition a disease, and more specifically it is theology that labels it a defect in reference to the intentions of God the Creator. Christian theology labels a genetic anomaly a "defect" when it is linked, through scientific research, with a condition similar to those that, according to the Gospels, Jesus acted to heal. Acting together, theology and genetic science can appropriately use the label "genetic defect" to speak of a genetic condition that is not merely painful or debilitating by human standards but is also contrary to God's intentions for the creation.

According to the Gospel accounts, Jesus acted to heal skin diseases, neurological disorders, and mental disorders (probably often labeled as demon possession), as well as the loss of hearing, sight, or the use of limbs, together with other unnamed diseases. Not surprisingly, we find little dissimilarity between the conditions Jesus healed and our modern concept of disease. After all, what caused pain, fear, and social rejection then often causes the same suffering today. But perhaps more important, the Gospel stories have so permeated the consciousness of our culture that through these stories our civilization has learned to define disease as that which Jesus healed, even after many have forgotten the source of the stories.

While the Gospel writers note that Jesus had pity or compassion on those he healed, the emphasis is on the cure or the healing, not the compassion. This is worth noting because often today, contemporary medicine is criticized as being stronger on curing than caring. For example, Stanley Hauerwas holds that for medicine "the constant temptation is to try to eliminate suffering through the agency of medicine rather than let medicine be the way we care for each other in our suffering" (1986, p. 17). If we look at the Gospels, however, we see that curing is not a temptation that diverts us from caring. On the contrary, healing is how compassion moves Jesus to act. This move to healing is central to the identity of Jesus, and thus it discloses the relationship between God and nature.

When we see how central these stories of healing are to the identity of Jesus in the Gospels, we are struck by how much healing has been ignored in modern theology. In the place of healing, modern theology has emphasized Jesus as the transformer of the human moral, spiritual, or social condition. We are more familiar with the relatively few stories of transformation (for example, Zaccheus's moral renewal or Jesus' protection of the woman caught in adultery) than we are of the stories of healing, which are far more frequent in the Gospel accounts. When stories involve both forgiveness of sins and healing, we concentrate our attention on the forgiveness of sins. Of course it is true that according to the Gospel stories, Jesus forgave sins and showed pity on those who suffered. But it is also true that according to these same stories, Jesus acted to heal. Without rejecting the portrait of Jesus as one who forgives or as one who shows mercy, we should focus on Jesus as one who heals, for it is this identity of Jesus as healer that grounds a Christian theology of medicine, include human genetic medicine. The stories of Jesus as healer establish our belief that God's redemptive work embraces the redemption of nature.

From the vantage point of a theology of the redemption of nature, it is possible to say that nature contains that which is defective *in reference to God's intentions*. Nature as a whole, regarded as God's creation, is good. But the goodness is marred by imperfection and distortion. This conviction, we have argued, is the only framework from which we can make sense of the healing activities of Jesus of Nazareth. Furthermore, within this framework we can consider specific aspects of nature as defective, not merely in reference to human desires or needs but also in reference to the intentions of the Creator. That which is defective is that which may be changed or altered. Indeed, altering it would be seen as an act of participation in the redemptive work of God.

The world is God's, yet it is not exactly what God intends, nor is it the home God intends for humanity. There is a moral gap between God's perfect intention and the creation's imperfect condition. It is within this moral gap between God's intention and creation's condition that Jesus healed the sick and fed the hungry. It is because of this moral gap that a redemption of nature is needed. Jesus intervened redemptively in nature to bring it into greater conformity with God's intentions.

It is also within this moral gap that our work and our technology are given room. Our work and our technology are offered as ways in which God brings the creation to conformity with God's intentions. If the world were exactly as God intends, it would be beyond moral improvement, and we would not be permitted to alter it, even if we wanted to. But the world is not what God intends, nor is it the home God intends for humanity. It is in this gap between divine intention and present condition that our technology is permitted to work. Through technology, as through all our action, we cooperate with God's redemptive intervention.

Christian theology has always seen redemption and restoration as God's work, offered by the Redeemer as a gift to the creation. Redemption lies beyond what the creation can do for itself and beyond what humanity can do for the rest of nature. God heals the creation until it is fully the creation that God intends: an earth without weeping or distress, premature death or violence (Isaiah 65:17–25). Christ brings forgiveness, healing, life, and new creation. This divine offer of redemption and restoration is to be met with humility and gratitude on our part. But God's action invites our response, both in cultivating the humility and faith of the new creation within ourselves and in doing the work of the new creation around us.

Just as God's redemptive work embraces both our human consciousness and the broader physical world, so our participation in God's redemptive work must extend to both dimensions. We are responsible for cultivating habits of thought, of worship, of humility, and of love. We are also to develop and practice techniques by which to reverse the disorder within nature.

Redemption and Technology

An active or technological spirituality, according to Christopher B. Kaiser, is solidly grounded in traditional Christian convictions:

> The early Christians believed in the possibility of healing and restoration that would truly benefit the needy. Underlying this belief was faith in a God who had created and could restore, a Messiah who had initiated God's final rule over both the forces of nature and the structures of society, and a Spirit who had been poured out on the believers enabling them to carry on the work of Jesus and to extend it to all nations. (1982, p. 15)

Kaiser credits Basil of Caesarea with the suggestion that the technical arts, including medicine, were given by God to human beings after the fall to "alleviate the harshness of nature" (1982, p. 20).

Augustine (354–430), the fountainhead of Western Christianity, praised technology:

> There are all the important arts discovered and developed by human genius, some for necessary uses, others simply for pleasure. Man shows remarkable powers of mind and reason in the satisfaction of his aims, even though they may be unnecessary, or even dangerous and harmful; and those powers are evidence of the blessings he enjoys in his natural powers which enable him to discover, to learn, and to practise those arts. Think of the wonderful inventions of clothing and building, the astounding achievements of human industry! Think of man's progress in agriculture and navigation. . . . Then there are all the weapons against his fellow-man in the shape of prisons, arms, and engines of war; all the medical resources for preserving or restoring health; all the seasonings or spices to gratify his palate or to tickle his appetite. Consider the multitudinous variety of the means of information and persuasion. (St. Augustine 1984 [*City of God* XXII 24], pp. 1072–73)

Because of its context, the implication of this passage is that God has given technological capability to human beings for them to use to ward off some of the effects of the fall.

Hugh of St. Victor, sometimes called the second Augustine, makes this suggestion explicit. Writing in the 1120s, Hugh says that human knowledge has two ends: "Either the restoring of our nature's integrity or the relieving of those weaknesses to which our present life lies subject" (*Didascalion* 1.5, quoted by Kaiser 1982, p. 20). The first goal, the repair of our integrity, is accomplished through the study of theology, mathematics, physics, ethics, economics, and politics. The second goal, the relief of our misery, is achieved through the mechanical arts, including agriculture and medicine (Kaiser 1982, pp. 20–21).

During the medieval Benedictine and Cluniac reforms, the saying *"ora et labora"* ("prayer and work") summarized an active spirituality. "Simply stated the principle claims that technological activity was a means of overcoming original sin" (Vaux 1970, p. 130). This form of spirituality was accompanied by widespread agricultural reforms and experiments that transformed the landscape of Europe and greatly increased the productivity of the land, contributing to the growth of cities and the rise of modern Europe. The Benedictines saw humanity as fallen, but more important, they saw it as their Christian duty not only to pray for salvation but also to apply their technical skill to a reversal of some of the effects of the fall. Just as sin was to be resisted, so were its effects: hunger, sickness, and death. Prayer and technology were both legitimate modes of service to God.

Undoing the damage of the fall was a motivation for early modern science and technology. Francis Bacon, the great advocate of experimental research, wrote, "For man by the fall fell at the same time from his state of innocency and from his dominion over creation. Both of these losses however can even in this life be in some part repaired; the former by religion and faith, the latter by arts and sciences" (1937 [1620], pp. 247–248). A century later John Wesley reiterated the theme: "But can nothing be found to lessen those inconveniences which cannot be wholly removed? To soften the evils of life, and prevent in part the sickness and pain to which we are continually exposed?" (1973 [1755], p. 10). Wesley answers that God has given us medicine and the ability to discover new techniques of healing.

In the poetry of John Milton the human struggle with nature was portrayed as both the glory and the tragedy of our existence. Struggling for survival in an often hostile environment has brought out the most brilliant and sometimes the most humane dimensions of our nature. In contrast to the easy, almost slothful existence of Adam and Eve in the garden, human struggle against a resistant nature is the loom upon which the tapestry of our accomplishments has been stretched. The traditional idea of the fall, then, is something of a mixed curse, for without it there would be no human endeavor, much less any divine redemption. David Daiches notes Milton's ambivalent feelings in describing the effects of the fall in *Paradise Lost*. The fall is tragic, and labor is cursed. But it is this curse that is the source of challenge and triumph. "Indeed, Milton has great difficulty in *Paradise Lost* in providing Adam and Eve with something to do, and he is clearly dissatisfied with their sole work of trimming a changeless garden" (Daiches 1984, p. 37). Re-making a garden out of a wilderness has been the most widespread form of redemptive technology for Christians throughout history. It is the fallenness of creation that gives occasion to the glory of work and to the beauty of cultivated fields at seedtime and harvest.

Genetic Engineering as Redemptive Technology

In the nineteenth century Horace Bushnell suggested various techniques of child rearing designed to improve the moral condition of the child. Bushnell, as we noted earlier, held to a Lamarckian view of evolution. He believed that child-rearing techniques would change a child's behavior in such a way that the alterations would be passed to the child's offspring. While Bushnell was wrong about transmission of acquired traits, it is revealing that he, as a leading popular theologian of his age, could advocate the use of the technology of child rearing for the purpose of improving the gene pool of the human race.

Today we are acquiring the capacity to do what Bushnell could only imagine, namely, to alter the genetic inheritance of organisms, human beings included, not merely by selection but by direct action. Should we think of this genetic alteration, or of attempts to alter the effects of genetic inheritance, as redemptive technology? Let us consider several specific potential uses of genetic engineering and ask to what extent they may be regarded as redemptive.

First, genetic engineering and analysis techniques will be used to study and to preserve genetic diversity of plants and animals, especially where these are threatened with extinction. The public rationale for this preservation of genetic diversity will be that it is prudent since our human future may depend in part on what we preserve. A theological rationale, fully compatible with the public rationale, may also be offered: Preservation of genetic diversity is a redemptive intervention because it reverses an immediate consequence of unwise human action.

Second, genetic engineering is being used to confer resistance to disease on agricultural plants, and to reduce their fertilizer needs. We may regard this as redemptive in that it enhances the usefulness of these plants while diminishing the environmental damage that has been part of their cultivation.

Third, genetic screening will become more widely available to couples concerned about the genetic health of their offspring. On the basis of screening, it is becoming possible to predict a couple's risk for conceiving a child with any of a growing number of genetic disorders. Some advocate widespread premarital genetic screening. A voluntary program among Jewish Americans screens couples considering marriage for Tay Sachs disease. The discovery in 1989 of one of the mutations that causes cystic fibrosis will create additional impetus for screening among whites. We may regard it as redemptive intervention if a couple is screened, found at serious risk, and advised not to conceive a child. Couples who accept this as redemptive on their part will also see it as costly, inasmuch as they forego the opportunity for offspring.

In some cases, it may become possible to assist couples at risk for conceiving a child with a genetic disorder to avoid this risk. For example, those at risk for X-linked disorders (such as hemophilia) may attempt to conceive in vitro and to have the conceptus analyzed genetically prior to implantation (Handyside, Kontogianni, Hardy, et al. 1990). It may become possible to expand this technique to handle a wider range of genetic disorders. The procedure results in a normal pregnancy, but at the cost of discarding unused and defective embryos (in the case of X-linked disorders, any male embryo is discarded). Anyone who regards the embryo as a human person will not find this technique acceptable. Those who reserve the category of personhood for a later stage of fetal development, however, may regard this as redemptive intervention.

Fourth, prenatal genetic testing will become increasingly widespread. In some cases, genetic diagnosis will lead to a course of therapy that will effectively treat the disease. In other cases, no therapy will be possible.

The only medical intervention will be abortion. Some will regard this intervention as purely destructive or wholly without redemptive meaning because it can only end life. Others will regard it as having a redemptive intention: the avoidance of a life of chronic disease. Any redemptiveness in this act is mixed with unavoidable loss.

Finally, in the next century, it may become possible to alter the genetic composition of a human embryo, removing a genetic defect from it and from its offspring. Such human germline therapy, so called because the therapeutic result is inherited, is far too risky with current technology. During the next two or three decades, as the technology develops, it will be important to encourage ethical and theological analysis of germline therapy. Is it prudent and responsible to make long-lasting alterations based upon our limited knowledge of genes and of their full effects? Is it a redemptive intervention, or is it shortsighted and likely to cause unforeseen and unwanted consequences?

In some of these examples, the use of genetic engineering opens redemptive possibilities for human action. In other examples, the mixture of healing and loss creates an ambiguous situation. Even when we share similar theological convictions, we may disagree among ourselves on whether intervention is truly redemptive in some of these situations. We will seek the guidance of our faith, agreeing that "faith is appropriate and intentional participation in the redemptive activity of God" (Dykstra 1986, p. 55). Our faith may lead us to conflicting conclusions and to different courses of action. Theology does not produce certainty or banish ambiguity. This fact, however, should not keep us from seeking to serve God's redemptive purposes through our technology. It should serve rather as a humbling reminder that redemption must always be taking place in us even as it takes place through us.

6

Participating in the Creation

In redeeming, God restores and heals that which has failed to attain its full creaturely goodness. In continuing to create, God calls new possibilities into existence. When we participate in redemption, we respond in compassion to that which is suffering and broken. When we participate in creation, we assist the unfolding of new dimensions of existence. Both redemption and creation are necessary to a comprehensive Christian theological understanding of God's relationship with nature. For that reason, an awareness of our participation in both creation and redemption is necessary to the theological framework in which we engage in genetic engineering. Without an understanding of redemption, we cannot see genetic engineering as therapy for that which is defective or damaged. Without an appreciation of creation, we cannot see genetic engineering as a creative exploration of the new.

In contrast to most of the theological responses to genetic engineering, I have argued that this technology must be seen in relationship to both redemption and creation. Having emphasized the relationship between genetic engineering and redemption, we are now ready to turn to the relationship between this technology and the work of God the Creator. We begin by considering the suggestion made by several theologians that technology be thought of as co-creation—that is, as human cooperation in creation. Several criticisms of this idea are made, although the term is not entirely rejected. Instead, the term is revised by considering how the biblical writers sometimes used technology as a metaphor for divine creativity. The suggestion is made that genetic engineering, in addition to the technologies of biblical times, may also be used as a metaphor for God's creative activity. Through an exploration of the logic of this metaphor, I argue that genetic engineering opens new possibilities for the future of God's creative work.

Genetic Engineering and Co-creation

After a period of relative neglect earlier in the twentieth century, the doctrine of creation has enjoyed a recent renaissance in Christian theology, probably due to an awakening of concern for our impact on the environment (Moltmann 1985). Before this current renaissance, the

Christian doctrine of creation emphasized creation in the beginning, and particularly the uniqueness of God's power to create *ex nihilo,* while human beings are always dependent on preexisting materials for our creative acts. More recent considerations of the doctrine of creation, however, have emphasized the continuing creativity of God, emphasizing the similarity between divine and human creativity through the recognition that God, like us, also creates by rearranging preexisting materials.

This renaissance in the doctrine of creation has been enriched by the contributions of theologians from a variety of perspectives. Important work has been done by Whiteheadian process theologians, notably John Cobb. Scientist-theologians such as Arthur Peacocke and John Polkinghorne have brought a thorough and rigorous appreciation of contemporary science into the discussion. Jürgen Moltmann has contributed a profound awareness of the relevance of traditional Christian beliefs, especially the doctrine of the Trinity. While these writers diverge widely in their assumptions and methods, they show a remarkable convergence in agreeing on these three affirmations: (1) Creation is an evolutionary process in which God is continuously active; (2) God is everywhere present, affecting the creation at every moment and at every level of complexity; and (3) the future of creation is uncertain, for God has not guaranteed its outcome. Taken together, these three affirmations summarize the doctrine of continuing creation or *creatio continua.*

As a result of nineteenth- and twentieth-century science, there is widespread agreement that nature is best understood as an evolutionary process. Cosmic evolution, from the initial singularity of the big bang through the birth and death of stars, and to the formation of planets such as Earth, has given rise to organic evolution and finally to a process of cultural evolution. Acceptance of this view leaves the idea of creation with two options: God may be seen as only the primordial architect of the big bang, or God may be seen as one who accompanies the evolution of the cosmos, sustaining and influencing its development (Peacocke 1979; Polkinghorne 1989). *Creatio continua,* of course, takes the second option.

This is not to say that the God who sustains and influences the creation is whimsical or erratic, defying the regularities of nature that are themselves grounded in God's origination of nature. While continuing to create, God respects both the stability and the freedom of what God has already created. Continuous creation is a divine action of influencing, of working through, of calling forth, and of offering new possibilities to all creatures. It is not a destruction of the old in order to begin anew.

Since God respects both the stabilities and the freedom of the creation, the course of future evolution is unknown. God influences but does not determine the future. God's influence elicits the response of the whole creation. Jürgen Moltmann has extended the idea of *creatio continua* to include the hope of a *creatio nova*, a new creation that is the consummation of all God's creative and redemptive acts. In the new creation, God is at home in the creation, and the purposes of God are fully expressed in nature. By continuing to create new forms and new possibilities, and by constantly redeeming all that is created, God is bringing about a new world in which the work of creation and redemption is one and complete.

Human beings, in particular, are capable of discerning the divine influence and of considering many ways in which to respond. So now we must ask: To what extent may we human beings, through our scientific understanding and our technological ability, serve God the Creator in this ongoing creativity? Human work, especially our technology, may be seen as a partnership with God in the continuing work of creation. Some have suggested the term "co-creation" to describe this role for humans. We have noted the use of the term in a 1983 statement on genetic engineering by the National Council of Churches (1984, p. 24–25). Kenneth Vaux makes extensive use of the term in his discussion of the human role in creation, understanding it to mean an ordering and even a subduing of the cosmos (Vaux 1970, pp. 121–22). Philip Hefner (1988, 1989) argues that we should think of ourselves as created co-creators: "The human being is God's created co-creator, whose purpose is the modifying and enabling of existing systems of nature so that they can participate in God's purposes in the mode of freedom" (1989, p. 212).

Recent Catholic thought, surrounding Pope John Paul's 1981 encyclical, *Laborem Exercens* (*On Human Work*), tends to affirm the language of co-creation. While the encyclical itself does not use the term, it does say: "Man shares by his work in the activity of the creator" (par. 25). Commenting on this theme, Michael Novak observes that here the Pope turns "to something rather deeper and more promising" than liberation theology (Novak 1983, p. 28). Liberation theology, of course, addresses the brokenness of work and the destructiveness of technology, motifs easily ignored in any discussion of co-creation that is not balanced with an emphasis on the need for redemption.

A helpful affirmation of the co-creation theme is offered by Arthur Peacocke (1979). While arguing that the idea of co-creation is part of the classic Hebrew and Christian perspectives, Peacocke adds that modern science and technology contribute in a major, substantive way in making the phrase point to an emerging capability. Through science, we have a far greater understanding of the natural processes through which God creates. We also understand, in far greater detail, the ecological interdependence of natural systems. With this knowledge comes a greater ability to interact, through technology, with nature. Through this increased knowledge of the very processes God uses in creating, and through increased ability to interact with these processes, human beings are now in a position to alter, for better or worse, the ongoing creative work of God.

> Man, with his new powers of technology and with new scientific knowledge of the ecosystems, if he chooses to acquire and apply it, could become that part of God's creation consciously and intelligently co-operating in the processes of creative change. . . . Man would then, through his science and technology, be exploring with God the creative possibilities within the universe God has brought into being. This is to see man as *co-explorer* with God. (Peacocke 1979, p. 306)

Understood this way, science and technology serve God's ongoing creative work. Together they offer God a new way to create and a new modality of divine agency in the physical world.

Despite the use of the term "co-creation" by a wide range of writers, the underlying concept contains several difficulties that should be recognized. First, it is not clear that we human beings can discern the purposes of God in creation, which we must be able to do if we are to cooperate with those purposes. Peacocke, who is optimistic about our ability to discern the purposes of God in nature through science, comments, "These themes, of co-creation and co-exploration, imply intelligent participation by man in God's work of creation. And for that God's meaning has to be discerned" (Peacocke 1979, p. 306; cf. p. 315). Can God's purposes be discerned through scientific comprehension of nature? Peacocke is quite explicit in answering affirmatively: "In man God has created through evolution a creature who is able to be aware of his (God's) purposes and to discern them and articulate them consciously" (Peacocke 1979, p. 301).

While science is certainly capable of understanding something about nature, it is quite another thing to claim that science is capable of discerning the purposes of the Creator. For example, science is able to identify the abnormal within nature (such as an infrequent gene), but it cannot make the judgment that the abnormal is defective, if we take defective to mean that which is contrary to divine intention. Science may see the link between a genetic abnormality and human suffering, but it cannot add that the abnormality and the suffering ought not to be, or that we have a right and an obligation to prevent them. One might argue equally on scientific grounds that abnormality is a good thing because it contributes to diversity.

Furthermore, science cannot discern God's intentions from nature unless it assumes, without warrant, that nature expresses God's intentions. As we have seen, central to the emerging notion of *creatio continua* is the awareness that nature is influenced but not determined by God, and that God is not finished with the creation. Since nature is only influenced by God and only partly completed, it cannot be held that nature fully reflects God's intentions. Even if science could attain perfect knowledge that really corresponds to the way the world is, science could not then infer God's will from the present condition of the world.

The notion of "co-creation" may be protected somewhat from this problem if we recognize the *noetic priority of redemption*. That is to say, we should begin our attempt to discern God's purposes in nature not with the scientific study of nature but with the theological question of the purpose of God disclosed through redemption. Redemption provides the necessary noetic clue to the interpretation of scientific insight. We see the purposes of God more clearly when we look at how God restores nature than when we look at nature itself. To understand the purposes of God in nature, Christian theology begins with the disclosure of those purposes in the relationship between Jesus and nature, a theme we have already explored. We should not expect to find that the God revealed in redemption will contradict the God revealed in nature and discerned through science. After all, the Christian tradition has always insisted that Creator and Redeemer are one in identity and purpose. Even so, the moral relationship between God and nature is not disclosed in nature. It is only discerned when we consider how God is redeeming nature.

The second problem of "co-creation" is the ambiguity inherent in the prefix. If "co-" is taken in the sense of a "co-worker," it suggests an equality that is wholly inappropriate to our relationship with God. As much as we might participate with God, we never have an equal role in that relationship. For this reason, Karl Barth rejects the language of "co-creation," seeing it as a threat to the divine prerogative. A person may participate in God's activity, but "this does not mean that he becomes a co-creator, a co-saviour or co-regent in God's activity. It does not mean that he becomes a kind of co-God" (Barth 1961 [1951], p. 482). Philip Hefner's "*created* co-creator" addresses this problem by clarifying the inherent subordination of the human role (1988, 1989). "Co-creation" can thus be explained so as to avoid the ambiguity of the prefix, but one wonders about the usefulness of a term that requires such obvious explanation.

Third, the characterization of human technology as "co-creation" is an inherently optimistic assessment. Such an assessment fails to recognize the disorder of nature, much less how this disorder permeates our intellect and our will, inevitably disordering our technology itself. One never reads of co-creation and sin in the same sentence. But our technology, for all its good, is constantly on the edge of sin, exploitation, and greed. It is, after all, *human* technology, beset by our weaknesses. To ignore this danger, as the language of co-creation so easily does, is to fail to guard against it. Not only are we *created* co-creators; we are creatures who constantly stand in need of redemption. If we may participate in God's creative and redemptive work, it is because we ourselves are being created and redeemed.

While it is proper to try to think about technology in relation to God's continuing work in creation, the idea of "co-creation" is inadequate by itself as a starting point. I am trying to revise the idea of co-creation by proposing two major changes. The first of these is to insist, as we have just done, that creation be joined with redemption. We are participants not only in creation but also in redemption. The second change, developed below, is to call attention to the metaphor implicit in the idea of co-creation and to explore the logic of this metaphor more fully, attempting to understand what it affirms about God as well as what it affirms about us and our technology.

Technology as Creation

The writers of the Hebrew scriptures often used technology to picture God's activity. They portrayed God as a gardener, an architect, a builder, and a potter (cf. Knight 1990). But they rarely portrayed God as a natural object or a natural process. The psalmist does not look to the hills for help, but to the God who *made* the hills (Psalm 121:1–2). In contrast to the cult of the Baal and the Asherah, the Hebrews worshiped Yahweh as the God who ruled over the processes of nature. The Baal and the Asherah were identified with biological and agricultural processes. They embodied fertility, and their worship was needed to bring fertility to the land. Yahweh, on the other hand, controlled fertility without being identified with it.

For centuries, the Hebrew worship of Yahweh and the Canaanite worship of the Baal and the Asherah existed side by side, and the Old Testament is full of references to the rivalry between the cults. Part of the theological struggle of the Old Testament writers is to portray Yahweh as a God both of exodus and of agriculture, capable of liberating the nation and of bringing fertility to land and herds and to the human family itself.

The Yahwist creation account (beginning in Genesis 2:4b) makes it clear that Yahweh is a God of agriculture. In this account, Yahweh creates the "earth creature" (Trible 1978) or "Adam" before anything else. No vegetation grows at first, and two reasons are given for this: "The Lord God had not caused it to rain upon the earth, and there was no man to till the ground" (Genesis 2:5, RSV). Yahweh had not provided rain (one of the functions of the Canaanite deities), and there was no human being to till the ground (Naidoff 1978). "Life is not possible, according to Genesis 2:5, without two critical elements: rainfall and human labor" (Meyers 1988, p. 83). Vegetation itself depends in part upon agriculture, which must wait until the human being is created.

After creating the human being or the earth creature, "the Lord God planted a garden in Eden, in the east; and there he put the man whom he had formed" (Genesis 2:8, RSV). Dramatically and explicitly, Yahweh is the first gardener. Gardening or agriculture is a metaphor for creation itself. After planting the garden, Yahweh places the human being in the garden with the command "to till it and keep it" (Genesis 2:15, RSV), thereby instructing the human being to emulate the divine work of creation. By authorizing human beings to practice gardening and agriculture, according to the Yahwist theology, God is authorizing human beings to create in the natural order. Indeed, by understanding vegetation as partly dependent upon agriculture, the Yahwist sees the human work of tilling the ground as something upon which God's own creative work depends. God as gardener depends in part on human gardeners to till and keep the garden.

This picture of God as gardener, together with other Old Testament portrayals of God as potter or builder, has at its core the claim that it is proper to say that "God works." Human work generally is taken as a picture of divine activity. That which is difficult to describe, namely, the action of God in creation, is portrayed through the everyday experience of human work.

Such language, of course, is metaphoric. Recently a number of scholars have considered the use of metaphor in religion and in other fields such as science (cf. Gerhart and Russell 1984; McFague 1987). We do not need to reiterate their findings here, but three points about metaphors should be noted as we seek to make religious use of metaphors drawn from technology.

First, a metaphor bridges two fields of meaning, taking a term from a familiar context to illuminate some aspect of experience that lies in a less familiar context. Thus we speak of sound waves and radio waves, connecting the movement of water, which is familiar, to the frequency patterns of sound and of radio transmissions, which we cannot see and which are therefore less familiar. When the Yahwist wrote that God planted a garden (Genesis 2:8), the familiar activity of planting was connected with the less familiar, unseen activity of God causing the earth to bear fruit. There is linguistic violence here (Gerhart and Russell 1984, p. 114). "God" and "planting" do not go together. Yet putting them together to say that "God planted a garden" expresses an important expansion of insight. In time, the community that forms itself around the Yahwist text recognizes the helpfulness of the insight: God causes the earth to bring forth vegetation. Any new metaphor bends language. Only over time can a community tell if the new language discloses an authentic insight.

By bridging between the familiar and the unfamiliar, a metaphor helps us picture what we cannot see. We cannot see God or the action of God. Through metaphors, however, we can picture God and God's activity. Without the ability to picture God through metaphors, we might be inclined to think that God is unseen and therefore unreal or inactive in creation. Human work, which is a sequence of actions aimed at a desired end, helps us to picture the involvement of God in the creation. Human technology, which typically depends upon the natural properties of other things, helps us to understand how God works through the natural properties of what God has created.

Second, when a metaphor creates a bridge from the familiar field of experience to the less familiar, it does not merge the two fields. Metaphors are self-limiting to a specific comparison of two terms. "God plants a garden" means only that God's activity can be thought of as something like planting; that is, God intentionally causes certain plants to grow in certain places. It does not mean that God is brought whole-sale into the human realm, as if God were a planter just like one of us, limited by all our constraints and working through the same techniques we must employ.

The full and unique richness of "God" remains uncompromised by the metaphor. In some Hebrew texts the verb *bara* is used uniquely to speak of God's act of creating; the same verb is not used to speak of human work. Later Jewish and Christian thought suggested that while humans can only create with preexisting material, God is not necessarily so limited. God creates by ordering or reshaping, which we do; but God also creates by bringing the stuff of the creation into existence, which we can never do. God creates both the material and its form out of nothing, or *ex nihilo*. While we are always limited by the constraints of the poten-tialities of the medium in which we work, God is not necessarily so limited or constrained. To say that God is a potter is not to say that God is necessarily limited by the properties of the clay, even though God freely respects the properties of what God has already created. The exis-tence of the clay and the specification of its properties are contingent upon the creative wisdom of God. We never create the medium in which we work, and we must first discover the medium's natural properties and learn to cooperate with them before we can achieve our desired ends. By contrast, God creates all media, assigning them their properties.

Third, a metaphor has a double significance or a rebounding meaning. God *plants:* This says something about the activity of God in relationship to plants. But a second meaning inevitably arises. If *God* plants, then our activity of planting takes on a new meaning, for we begin to see ourselves as participating in an activity of God. By saying (metaphori-cally) that God does what we do, we begin to see ourselves doing what God does. Some of the richness of "God" is now attached to our humble activity of planting. To say that God is a potter tells us something about God, but it also reforms our idea of the work of the potter. We now see the human potter's work as a mode of divine activity, as a form of partici-pation in God's work, as a bringing of form to matter, and as a devotion to beauty, grace, and utility in everyday objects.

It is on the basis of this rebounding meaning that it is possible to speak of human work as participation in the work of God. Through metaphoric extension and return, our work takes on new and rich meaning. Through metaphoric *extension*, we envision God doing something we do. Through metaphoric rebound, we see our own activity all over again, in a new light, as something God does. Through this metaphoric process, the meaning of our activity has been transformed and enriched by its metaphoric use, and so we try to live up to its new meaning, doing our work as we envision God doing it. It may be true that our work, considered on its own terms, lacks dignity or meaning (Hauerwas 1983). But when our work is the major source of metaphors for God's action in creation and redemption, meaning and dignity flow into our work through the rebound of metaphor. Our work's dignity does not spring from our worth or from the success of our accomplishments but from the activity of God in whose work our work is found.

When we picture God working through a specific technology, we confer a value and a legitimacy upon that technology. For example, if God is seen as one who plants a garden, then the human activity of planting is given value and legitimacy. This means that it is permissible for us to engage in the activity, and even that we are doing something worthy when we do so. It lends support to our creativity and to our desire to develop new techniques of gardening. If God works through this technology, then we want the technology to be an increasingly efficient and productive mode of divine activity.

More important, if we believe that God works through this technology, then we want our purposes to coincide with God's purposes. Why does God plant a garden? To bring beauty to the earth, to create diversity, to provide food, and to make a habitable planet for other creatures (Genesis 2:9). Why do we plant gardens and restore forests? For the same reasons. And when we do so, we see ourselves cooperating with God, offering our work as an extension of the Creator's work.

It may be, of course, that we cannot see God as active in a particular technology or project. Such a technology or project is somehow inconsistent with the nature of God or with the other ways in which we see God. If that is the case, then it should also be true that we should not engage in the activity ourselves. "Unless the Lord builds the house, those who build it labor in vain" (Psalms 127:1, RSV). Only when we can recognize the activity of God in our human work is it proper for us to proceed. If we cannot imagine God, metaphorically, working by means of a particular technology, then we should refrain from that technology. If we cannot see the activity of God in a particular project, then we should not be involved. Unless our work is consistent with the character and the activity of God, our labor is in vain, without personal meaning and without any contribution to a broader purpose. It is countercreative and counterredemptive.

Genetic Engineering as Creation

The biblical writers saw God creating through the technologies of their day. Are today's technologies theologically different? Is it possible for us to see God creating through our most sophisticated research and development? Compared to the technology of the biblical era, our skills are far more powerful, and they are based on research. But these reasons do not alienate our technology from the Creator. On the contrary, they should increase our urgency as we move to reconnect God and technology. As technology grows in scope and power, a God alienated from it is diminished in our thinking, and technology knows no theological limit.

Rarely have recent theological and liturgical writers connected God and technology. This silence reinforces the notion that modern technology is alien to God, perhaps even God's enemy or a demon. The practical result is that traditional technologies (such as farming) are seen as proper, but new technologies are taken to be foreign to God, and those who engage in them are often seen as running the risk of being irreligious. If we are unable to imagine God as working through new technologies, we maintain a wall of separation between them and God. By our lack of theological imagination (when compared to the biblical writers), we nudge God out of our modern consciousness. The technologies of our age are pursued without reference to God, and there is no theological foundation upon which we can see technology or science as a Christian vocation.

References to today's technologies are largely absent from liturgy, sermons, and theological literature. Perhaps the rapid expansion of technology has simply overwhelmed the capacity of religious writers. Perhaps religious writers do not understand technology, or assume that their readers do not, and so avoid references to it. Metaphors, after all, communicate meaning only when writer and reader both understand the original context of a term. To say meaningfully that God is a potter requires that both writer and reader know what a potter is. With technology developing rapidly on many fronts, few have an understanding of what engineers or technologists do. An irony of our age is that as technology grows in power, fewer of us understand it or experience the methods of research and production first hand.

This lack of familiarity makes the theological task not only more difficult but also more urgent. Can we learn to speak of God and technology with the same ease with which biblical writers connected the divine with the human? In particular, can we speak of God and genetic engineering? If the Yahwist could say that God planted a garden, can we not say that God engages in genetic engineering?

When the question is put this way, some might immediately try to picture God adding restriction enzymes to a DNA sample. In other words, some will take the metaphorical language literally, as if God were engaged in genetic engineering in just the same way as the human researcher in a genetics laboratory. But this disregards both the linguistic form of metaphor and the uniqueness of divine activity. God plants a garden: God causes vegetation to cover the earth without digging holes.

different level / human intervention

God engages in genetic engineering: God seeks intentional genetic change but does not mix the contents of test tubes.

Provided we are careful to speak metaphorically, with full regard for the limits as well as the affirmation of meaning, is it appropriate to say that God engages in what amounts to the same thing as genetic engineering? Can we picture the creativity of God through the metaphor of our own abilities to alter genetic materials?

An affirmative answer is consistent with the convictions of the Christian tradition through the centuries. It represents an important and decisive *expansion* of this traditional perspective, but it is not inconsistent with it. It has always been part of the Christian tradition to affirm that God works through the creation, using all natural processes and the activities of humans to extend that divine activity in the creation. More recently, it has been said that that God works through the basic processes described by biology, processes such as genetic mutation, recombination, and selection, processes through which we too can now act.

natural / al / natural

We have noted that genetic engineering uses the natural processes of genetic recombination that have existed in nature for several billion years. Without these natural processes of genetic recombination across lines of descent, evolution would be such a slow process that we (along with most other organisms) could not have yet evolved. Now that we understand these processes, we have begun to use them. Our use of these processes gives us a way to picture how God has been working through them over the past billions of years. We surely do not want to say that God has been uninvolved all along in these molecular processes. Such a restriction would greatly limit what we would mean by the creative work of God. But until recently, we have not understood these processes or how they can be altered intentionally. With this new understanding, we can affirm something more about the Creator. Saying metaphorically that God engages in genetic engineering is simply another way to picture God's patient involvement in the fine detail of the evolution of life.

It is also an affirmation that our genetic engineering has the potential for being an extension of the work of God. If we agree that God works through the natural processes themselves, is God's activity pushed back simply because we humans have learned to use these processes? God does not cease to work through these biological processes simply because humans have begun to use them. Genetic engineering does not encroach upon the scope of divine activity. It expands the reach of God's action, placing a new mode of contact, through our technology, between the Creator and the creation. God now has more ways create, to redeem, and to bring the creation to fulfillment and harmony. Human beings who seek to serve God through genetic engineering are placing new instruments, namely, their technical skill, into the hands of the Creator.

By continually creating new forms and new realities, God is continuing to unfold the evolution of the universe and the evolution of life on our planet. There is no limit to the possibilities of what God may yet create. And by continually redeeming the creation from its brokenness and sin, by restoring relationship, and by renewing all things, God is transforming this evolving cosmos so that it will fully express God's purposes and God's glory.

We are in the midst of this creative and redemptive passage from creation in the beginning to the consummation of all things in the new creation. We ourselves are being created and redeemed, for we are destined to be part of the new creation God is making. But we are more than passive observers, for God has called us to participate in this creative and redemptive transformation of the creation. Certainly it is true that we humans can use genetic engineering for ends that confound the purposes and defy the glory of God. These natural processes sometimes conflict with God's purposes even without our help. But when through genetic engineering these processes are used by human beings to expand the purposes and the glory of God, must it not be said that genetic engineering is an extension of God's activity?

When I say metaphorically that God engages in genetic engineering, I mean this:

—God seeks genetic change as a proper means of creative and redemptive activity.
—God works through natural processes to achieve genetic change.
—God works through humans to achieve intentional genetic change.
—The genetic engineering in which God engages, and to which our involvement should be limited, is that which is consistent with the nature and purposes of God the Creator and Redeemer, who renews the whole creation in anticipation of a new creation.

Long before our arrival on earth, God the Creator was at work through microbiological processes. Through billions of years of creation, God has opened up the creation for a stunning diversity of species. Working through untold instances of mutation, recombination, and natural selection, God has drawn out the creation patiently, step by step. Only in the most recent moment of creation have we appeared, and already our technology is giving us the power to add to this great work of creation.

and vast, extenction, grooping

References

Alexander, Richard D. 1987. *The Biology of Moral Systems*. Hawthorne, N.Y.: Aldine de Gruyter.

Augustine of Hippo. 1984. *City of God*. Trans. Henry Bettenson. New York: Penguin Books.

Ayala, Francisco Jose, and Theodosius Dobzhansky, eds. 1974. *Studies in the Philosophy of Biology*. Berkeley: University of California Press.

Bacon, Francis. 1937. [1620.] Magna Instauratio. In *Essays, Advancement of Learning, New Atlantis, and other Pieces*, ed. Richard Foster Jones. New York: Odyssey Press.

Bailey, J. Michael, and Richard C. Pillard. 1991. A genetic study of male sexual orientation. *Archives of General Psychiatry* 48:1089–96.

Barbour, Ian G. 1966. *Issues in Science and Religion*. New York: Harper Torchbooks.

Barrow, John D., and Frank J. Tipler. 1986. *The Anthropic Cosmological Principle*. New York: Oxford University Press.

Barth, Karl. 1961. [1951.] *Church Dogmatics* III/4. Trans. A. T. Mackay, T. H. L. Parker, Harold Knight, Henry A. Kennedy, and John Marks. Edinburgh: T. & T. Clark.

Becker, Carl L. 1932. *The Heavenly City of the Eighteenth-Century Philosophers*. New Haven, Conn.: Yale University Press.

Berg, Paul, David Baltimore, Herbert W. Boyer, Stanley N. Cohen, Ronald W. Davis, David S. Hogness, Daniel Nathans, Richard Roblin, James D. Watson, Sherman Weissman, and Norton D. Zinder. 1974. Potential biohazards of recombinant DNA molecules. *Science* 185:303.

Bertranpetit, J., and L. L. Cavalli-Sforza. 1991. A genetic reconstruction of the history of the population of the Iberian peninsula. *Annals of Human Genetics* 55:51–67.

Blum, Kenneth, E. P. Noble, P. J. Sheridan, Anne Montgomery, Terry Ritchie, Pudur Jagadeeswaran, Harou Nogami, Arthur H. Briggs, and Jay B. Cohn. 1990. Allelic association of the human dopamine D_2 receptor gene in alcoholism. *Journal of the American Medical Association* 263:2055–60.

Bolos, Annabel M., Michael Dean, Susan Lucas-Derse, Mark Ramsburg, Gerald L. Brown, and David Goldman. 1990. Population and pedigree studies reveal a lack of association between the dopamine D_2 receptor gene and alcoholism. *Journal of the American Medical Association* 264:3156–60.

Boserup, Ester. 1970. *Women's Role in Economic Development*. London: Allen & Unwin.

Bouchard, Claude, Angelo Tremblay, Jean-Pierre Despres, André Nadeau, Paul J. Lupien, Germain Theriault, Jean Dussault, Sital Moorjani, Sylvie Pinault, and Guy Fournier. 1990. The response to long-term overfeeding in identical twins. *The New England Journal of Medicine* 322:1477–82.

Bouchard, Thomas J., Jr., David T. Lykken, Matthew McGue, Nancy L. Segal, and Aake Tellegen. 1990. Sources of human psychological differences: The Minnesota study of twins reared apart. *Science* 250:223–28.

Brungs, Robert A., S.J. 1983. Biotechnology: A new reality. *Listening* 18:275–83.

Bultmann, Rudolf. 1951, 1955. *Theology of the New Testament*. 2 vols. Trans. K. Grobel. New York: Charles Scribner's Sons.

Bushnell, Horace. 1903. [1858.] *Nature and the Supernatural as Together Constituting the One System of God*. New York: Charles Scribner's Sons.
———. 1903. [1888.] *Christian Nurture*. New York: Charles Scribner's Sons.

Cann, Rebecca L., Mark Stoneking, and Allan C. Wilson. 1987. Mitochondrial DNA and human evolution. *Nature* 325:31–36.

Capecchi, Mario R. 1989a. Altering the genome by homologous recombination. *Science* 244:1288–92.

Carter, Jack L., Frank Heppner, Roy H. Saigo, Geraldine Twitty, and Dan Walter. 1990. The state of the biology major. *BioScience* 40:678–83.

Chakraborty, Ranajit, and Kenneth K. Kidd. 1991. The utility of DNA typing in forensic work. *Science* 254:1735–39.

Chargaff, E. 1976. On the dangers of genetic meddling. *Science* 192:938.

Cherfas, Jeremy. 1990. Molecular biology lies down with the lamb. *Science* 249:124–26.

Corea, Gena. 1985. *The Mother Machine: Reproductive Technologies from Artificial Insemination to Artificial Wombs*. New York: Harper & Row.

Culliton, Barbara. 1989. Gene test begins. *Science* 244:913.

Daiches, David. 1984. *God and the Poets*. The Gifford Lectures, 1983. Oxford: Clarendon Press.

Darwin, Charles. 1968. [1859.] *On the Origin of Species by Means of Natural Selection*. Baltimore: Penguin Books.

Davis, Bernard D. 1977. The recombinant DNA scenarios: Andromeda strain, chimera, and golem. *American Scientist* 65:547–55.
———. 1980. Frontiers of the biological sciences. *Science* 209:78–89.

Davis, Bernard D., and H. Tristram Engelhardt, Jr. 1984. Genetic engineering: Prospects and recommendations. *Zygon* 19:277–80.

Dawkins, Richard. 1976. *The Selfish Gene*. Oxford: Oxford University Press.

Dickson, David. 1989. Genome project gets rough ride in Europe. *Science* 243:599.

Dobzhansky, Theodosius, F. J. Ayala, G. L. Stebbins, and J. W. Valentine. 1977. *Evolution*. San Francisco: W. H. Greeman.

Dobzhansky, Theodosius, and Ernest Boesiger. 1983. *Human Culture: A Moment in Evolution*. Ed. Bruce Wallace. New York: Columbia University Press.

Dykstra, Craig. 1986. What is faith? An experiment in the hypothetical mode. In *Faith Development and Fowler*, ed. Craig Dykstra and Sharon Parks. Birmingham, Ala.: Religious Education Press.

Eliade, Mircea. 1962. *The Forge and the Crucible*. Trans. S. Corrin. London: Rider and Co.

———. 1963. *Patterns in Comparative Religion*. Trans. Rosemary Sheed. Cleveland: World Publishing Co.

———. 1978. *History of Religious Ideas*. Vol. 1, *From the Stone Age to the Eleusinian Mysteries*. Trans. Willard R. Trask. Chicago: University of Chicago Press.

Episcopal Church. 1985. Resolution on genetic engineering research. *Journal*, House of Bishops, pp. 179–180. New York.

Erlich, Henry A., David Gelfand, and John J. Sninsky. 1991. Recent advances in the polymerase chain reaction. *Science* 252:1643–51.

Ezzell, Carol. 1987. EPA clears the way for release of nitrogen-fixing microbe. *Nature* 327:90.

———. 1989. Transgenic sticky issues. *Nature* 338:366.

Foundation on Economic Trends. 1983. *Resolution*. Washington, D.C.: Foundation on Economic Trends.

Friedmann, Theodore. 1989. Progress toward human gene therapy. *Science* 244:1275–81.

Gasson, Charles S., and Robert T. Fraley. 1989. Genetically engineering plants for crop improvement. *Science* 244:1293–99.

Gerhart, Mary, and Allan Russell. 1984. *Metaphoric Process: The Creation of Scientific and Religious Understanding*. Fort Worth: Texas Christian University Press.

Gibbons, Ann. 1990a. Biotechnology takes root in the Third World. *Science* 248:962–63.

———. 1990b. Our chimp cousins get that much closer. *Science* 250:376.

———. 1991a. Looking for the father of us all. *Science* 251:378–80.

———. 1991b. Systematics goes molecular. *Science* 251:872–74.

Gustafson, James M. 1981, 1984. *Ethics from a Theocentric Perspective*. 2 vols. Chicago: University of Chicago Press.

Handyside, A. H., E. H. Kontogianni, K. Hardy, and R. M. L. Winston. 1990. Pregnancies from biopsied human preimplantation embryos sexed by Y-specific DNA amplifications. *Nature* 344:768–70.

Hastings Center Report . 1989. [Note.] *Hastings Center Report* 19:48.

Hauerwas, Stanley. 1983. Work as co-creation: A critique of a remarkably bad idea. In *Co-Creation and Capitalism: John Paul II's Laborem Exercens,* ed. John W. Houck and Oliver F. Williams, C.S.C. Lanham, Md.: University Press of America.

———. 1986. *Suffering Presence: Theological Reflections on Medicine, the Mentally Handicapped, and the Church.* Notre Dame, Ind.: University of Notre Dame Press.

Hefner, Philip. 1988. Theology's truth and scientific formulation. *Zygon* 23:263–79.

———. 1989. The evolution of the created co-creator. In *The Cosmos as Creation: Theology and Science in Consonance,* ed. T. Peters. Nashville: Abingdon Press.

Heiser, Charles B., Jr. 1973. *Seeds to Civilization: The Story of Man's Food.* San Francisco: W. H. Freeman.

Hick, John. 1966. *Evil and the God of Love.* New York: Harper & Row.

Hoffman, Michelle. 1991. Unraveling the genetics of fragile X syndrome. *Science* 252:1070.

Hoffman, Stephen L., Victor Nussenzweig, Jerald C. Sadoff, and Ruth S. Nussenzweig. 1991. Progress toward malaria preerythrocytic vaccines. *Science* 252:520–521.

Holden, Constance. 1991a. New center to study therapies and ethnicity. *Science* 251:748.

———. 1991b. Probing the complex genetics of alcoholism. *Science* 251:163–64.

Hotchkiss, Rollin D. 1965. Portents for a genetic engineering. *Journal of Heredity* 56:197–202.

Howard, Ted, and Jeremy Rifkin. 1977. *Who Should Play God?* New York: Dell Publishing Co.

Huxley, Julian. 1947. [1943.] Evolutionary ethics. In *Evolution and Ethics 1893–1943,* by T. H. Huxley and Julian Huxley. London: Pilot Press.

Huxley, T. H. 1947. [1893.] Evolution and ethics. In *Evolution and Ethics 1893–1943,* by T. H. Huxley and Julian Huxley. London: Pilot Press.

Hybridomas: The making of a revolution. 1982. *Science* 215:1074.

John Paul II. 1981. *Laborem Exercens.* Rome: Vatican.

———. 1982. Biological research and human dignity. *Origins* 12:342–43.

———. 1983. The ethics of genetic manipulation. *Origins* 13:385–89.

———. 1987. Instruction on respect for human life in its origin and on the dignity of procreation. *Origins* 16:697–711.

Kaiser, Christopher. 1982. The early Christian belief in creation: Background for the origins and assessment of modern Western science. *Horizons in Biblical Theology* 9:1–30.

Kee, Howard Clark. 1986. *Medicine, Miracle and Magic in New Testament Times.* Cambridge: Cambridge University Press.

Knight, Douglas. 1990. Ancient Israelite cosmology. In *The Church and Contemporary Cosmology,* ed. James B. Miller and Kenneth E. McCall. Pittsburgh: Carnegie Mellon University Press.

Kolata, Gina. 1984. Scrutinizing sleeping sickness. *Science* 226:956–59.

Lamb, Chris, and Leona Fitzmaurice. 1986. Tailoring crop improvement. *Nature* 324:414.

Lamming, G. E. 1988. Regulating growth in animals. *Nature* 336:19–20.

Lappe, Marc. 1984. *Broken Code: The Exploitation of DNA.* San Francisco: Sierra Club Books.

Lewontin, R. C., and Daniel L. Hartl. 1991. Population genetics in forensic DNA typing. *Science* 253:1745–50.

McFague, Sallie. 1987. *Models of God: Theology for an Ecological, Nuclear Age.* Philadelphia: Fortress Press.

Marx, Jean L. 1988a. Gene-watcher's feast served up in Toronto. *Science* 242:32–33.

————. 1988b. Gene transfer is coming on target. *Science* 242:191–92.

————. 1990. Dissecting the complex diseases. *Science* 247:1540–42.

Meyers, Carol. 1988. *Discovering Eve: Ancient Israelite Women in Context.* New York: Oxford University Press.

Milstein, C., and G. Kohler. 1975. Continuous cultures of fused cells secreting antibody of predefined specificity. *Nature* 256:495.

Moltmann, Jürgen. 1985. *God in Creation: A New Theology of Creation and the Spirit of God.* The Gifford Lectures 1984–1985. Trans. M. Kohl. San Francisco: Harper & Row.

Moss, Bernard. 1991. Vaccinia virus: A tool for research and vaccine development. *Science* 252:1662–67.

Naidoff, Bruce D. 1978. A man to work the soil: A new interpretation of Genesis 2–3. *Journal for the Study of the Old Testament* 5:2–14.

National Academy of Sciences. 1975. *Underexploited Tropical Plants with Promising Economic Value.* Washington, D.C.: National Academy of Sciences.

National Council of the Churches of Christ. 1980. *Human Life and the New Genetics.* New York: National Council of the Churches of Christ.

————. 1984. [1983.] *Genetic Engineering: Social and Ethical Consequences.* New York: Pilgrim Press.

————. 1986. *Genetic Science for Human Benefit.* New York: National Council of the Churches of Christ.

Nelson, J. Robert. 1984. *Human Life.* Philadelphia: Fortress Press.

————. 1990. The role of religions in the analysis of the ethical issues of human gene therapy. *Human Gene Therapy* 1:43–48.

New York Times. 1989. Genetic tracking of criminals is urged by California official. *New York Times,* April 8, pp. 1, 8.

Norman, Colin. 1983. Clerics urge ban on altering germline cells. *Science* 220:1360–61.

Novak, Michael. 1983. Creation theology. In *Co-Creation and Capitalism: John Paul II's Laborem Exercens,* ed. John W. Houck and Oliver F. Williams, C.S.C. Lanham, Md.: University Press of America.

Overall, Christine. 1987. *Ethics and Human Reproduction: A Feminist Analysis.* Boston: Allen & Unwin.

Palmiter, Richard D., Ralph L. Brinster, Robert E. Hammer, Myra E. Trumbauer, Michael G. Rosenfeld, Neal C. Birnberg, and Ronald M. Evans. 1982. Dramatic growth of mice that develop from eggs microinjected with metallothionein-growth hormone fusion genes. *Nature* 300:611–15.

Parsegian, V. L. 1973. Biological trends within cosmic processes. *Zygon* 8:221–43.

Peacocke, Arthur R. 1979. *Creation and the World of Science.* The Bampton Lectures, 1978. Oxford: Clarendon Press.

Plomin, Robert. 1990. The role of inheritance in behavior. *Science* 248:183–88.

Polkinghorne, John. 1989. *Science and Providence.* Cambridge: Cambridge University Press.

President's Commission for the Study of Ethical Problems in Medicine and Biomedical and Behavioral Research. 1982. *Splicing Life: A Report on the Social and Ethical Issues of Genetic Engineering with Human Beings.* Washington, D.C.: U.S. Government Printing Office.

Pursel, Vernon G., Carl A. Pinkert, Kurt F. Miller, Douglas J. Bolt, Roger G. Campbell, Richard D. Palmiter, Ralph L. Brinster, and Robert E. Hammer. 1989. Genetic engineering of livestock. *Science* 244:1281–88.

Rahner, Karl. 1966a. The experiment with man: Theological observations on man's self-manipulation. In *Theological Investigations IX*, pp. 205–24. Trans. G. Harrison. New York: Seabury.

———. 1966b. The problem of genetic manipulation. In *Theological Investigations IX*, pp. 225–52. Trans. G. Harrison. New York: Seabury.

Ramsey, Paul. 1970. *Fabricated Man: The Ethics of Genetic Control.* New Haven, Conn.: Yale University Press.

Ravin, Arnold W. 1977. On natural and human selection, or saving religion. *Zygon* 12:27–41.

Rifkin, Jeremy. 1983. *Algeny.* New York: Penguin Books.

Rindos, David. 1984. *The Origins of Agriculture: An Evolutionary Perspective.* Orlando, Fla.: Academic Press.

Roberts, Leslie. 1988b. New targets for human gene therapy. *Science* 241:906.

———. 1990a. An animal genome project? *Science* 248:550–52.

———. 1990b. Cystic fibrosis corrected in lab. *Science* 249:1503.

———. 1990c. Down to the wire for the NF gene. *Science* 249:236–38.

———. 1990d. New scissors for cutting chromosomes. *Science* 249:127.

———. 1991. A genetic survey of vanishing peoples. *Science* 252:1614–17.

Rosenfeld, Melissa A., Wolfgang Siegfried, Kunihiko Yoshimura, Koichi Yoneyama, Masashi Fukayama, Larue E. Stier, Paavo K. Pääkkö, Pascale Gilardi, Leslie D. Stratford-Perricaudet, Michel Perricaudet, Sophie Jallat, Andrea Pavirani, Jean-Pierre Lecocq, and Ronald G. Crystal. 1991. Adenovirus-mediated transfer of a recombinant $\alpha 1$-antitrypsin gene to the lung epithelium in vivo. *Science* 252:431–34.

Sagan, Carl, Hans A. Bethe, S. Chandrasekhar, et al. 1990. *Perserving and Cherishing the Earth: An Appeal for Joint Commitment in Science and Religion.* Moscow.

Schwarz, Hans. 1970. Theological implications of modern biogenetics. *Zygon* 5:247–68.

Science magazine (author not known). 1988. Fingerprinting takes the witness stand. 240:1616–18.

———. 1989a. Human Genome Project. 243:167.

———. 1991a. Germ cell gene panel. 253:841.

———. 1991b. On the trail of genes for IQ. 252:1352.

Shinn, Roger Lincoln. 1982. *Forced Options: Social Decisions for the 21st Century.* San Francisco: Harper & Row.

Sinsheimer, Robert L. 1975. Troubled dawn for genetic engineering. *New Scientist* 16:148.

———. 1983. Genetic engineering: Life as a plaything. *Technology Review* 86:14–17,70.

Smith, H. Shelton. 1955. *Changing Conceptions of Original Sin.* New York: Charles Scribner's Sons.

Sokal, Robert R., Neal L. Oden, and Chester Wilson. 1991. Genetic evidence for the spread of agriculture in Europe by demic diffusion. *Nature* 351:143–45.

Strom, Charles, Yury Verlinsky, Svetlana Milayeva, et al. 1990. Preconception genetic diagnosis of cystic fibrosis. *The Lancet* 336:306–7.

Tennant, F. R. 1902. *The Origin and Propagation of Sin.* Cambridge: University Press.

Toulmin, Stephen. 1970. [1957.] Contemporary scientific mythology. In *Metaphysical Beliefs: Three Essays by S. Toulmin, R. Hepburn, and A. MacIntyre.* New York: Schocken Books.

Townes, Charles. 1988. On science, and what it might suggest about us. *Theological Education* 25:7–21.

Trible, Phyllis. 1978. *God and the Rhetoric of Sexuality.* Philadelphia: Fortress Press.

United Church of Christ. 1989. *The Church and Genetic Engineering.* New York: United Church of Christ.

United Methodist Church Genetic Science Task Force. 1991. Draft report to Annual and Central Conferences, December, 1990. *Christian Social Action,* 1991 (January):17–27.

United States Catholic Conference. 1977. The implications of recombinant DNA. *Origins* 6:771–72.

Vaux, Kenneth. 1970. *Subduing the Cosmos: Cybernetics and Man's Future.* Richmond, Virginia: John Knox Press.

Waddington, C. H. 1941. [1948.] *The Scientific Attitude.* 2nd ed. Middlesex: Penguin Books.

Wade, Nicholas. 1977. *The Ultimate Experiment: Man-Made Evolution.* New York: Walker and Co.

Ward, Keith. 1982. *Rational Theology and the Creativity of God.* New York: Pilgrim Press.

Wertz, Dorothy C., and John C. Fletcher. 1989. Fatal knowledge: Prenatal diagnosis and sex selection. *Hastings Center Report* 19:21–27.

Wesley, John. 1973. [1755.] *Primitive Remedies.* Santa Barbara, Calif.: Woodbridge Press.

———. 1978. [1756.] The doctrine of original sin, according to scripture, reason, and experience. In *The Works of John Wesley,* vol. 9. Grand Rapids, Mich.: Baker Book House.

Williams, George C. 1988. Huxley's evolution and ethics in sociobiological perspective. *Zygon* 23:383–407.

Wilson, Edward O. 1975. *Sociobiology: The New Synthesis.* Cambridge: Harvard University Press.

Womack, James E. 1987. Genetic engineering in agriculture: Animal genetics and development. *Trends in Genetics* 3:65–68.

World Council of Churches. 1975. *Genetics and the Quality of Life.* Geneva: World Council of Churches.

———. 1982. *Manipulating Life.* Geneva: World Council of Churches.

———. 1989. *Biotechnology: Its Challenges to the Churches and the World.* Geneva: World Council of Churches.

Zahn-Waxler, Carolyn, E. Mark Cummings, and Ronald Iannotti, eds. 1986. *Altruism and Aggression: Biological and Social Origins.* Cambridge: Cambridge University Press.

Zeuner, Friedrich Eberhard. 1963. *History of Domesticated Animals.* New York: Harper & Row.

Zuckerman, Marvin. 1990. Some dubious premises in research and theory of racial differences: Scientific, social, and ethical issues. *American Psychologist* 45:1297–1303.

Recommended Reading

Agius, Emmanuel. 1989. Germline Cells: Our Responsibilities for Future Generations. In *Ethics in the Natural Sciences*, ed. Dietmar Mieth and Jacques Pohier (English language ed. P. Hillyer), pp. 105–15. Edinburgh: T. & T. Clark.

Anderson, Bernard Word. 1957. *Understanding the Old Testament*. Englewood Cliffs, N.J.: Prentice-Hall.

Anderson, W. French. 1984. Prospects for human gene therapy. *Science* 226:401–9.

Benz, Ernst. 1968. [1965.] *Evolution and Christian Hope: Man's Concept of the Future from the Early Fathers to Teilhard de Chardin*. Trans. H. Frank. Garden City, New York: Doubleday Anchor Books.

Borowski, Oded. 1987. *Agriculture in Iron Age Israel*. Winona Lake, Ind.: Eisenbrauns.

Brill, Winston J. 1985. Safety concerns and genetic engineering in agriculture. *Science* 227:381–84.

Browning, Peter. 1982. Ethical options of the new genetics. *Church & Society* 73:52–61.

Brueggemann, Walter. 1977. *The Land: Place as Gift, Promise, and Challenge in Biblical Faith*. Philadelphia: Fortress Press.

Brungs, Robert A. 1989. *You See Lights Breaking Upon Us: Doctrinal Perspectives on Biological Advance*. St. Louis: Robert A. Brungs.

Buber, Martin. 1949. *The Prophetic Faith*. Trans. C. Witton-Davies. New York: Macmillan.

Capecchi, Mario R. 1989. The new mouse genetics: Altering the genome by gene targeting. *Trends in Genetics* 5:70–76.

Cole-Turner, Ronald S. 1987. Is genetic engineering co-creation? *Theology Today* 44:338–49.

———. 1989. Genetic engineering: Our role in creation. In *The New Faith-Science Debate*, ed. J. Mangum, pp. 68–75. Minneapolis: Fortress Press.

Curtis, Adrian. 1985. *Ugarit (Ras Shamra)*. Grand Rapids, Mich.: Eerdmans.

Dearman, John Andrew. 1988. *Property Rights in the Eighth-Century Prophets: The Conflict and Its Background*. Atlanta: Scholars Press.

Dobzhansky, Theodosius. 1967. *The Biology of Ultimate Concern*. New York: The New American Library.

———. 1973. Ethics and values in biological and cultural evolution. *Zygon* 8:261–81.

Dubos, Rene. 1980. *The Wooing of Earth*. New York: Charles Scribner's Sons.

Engelhardt, H. Tristram, Jr. 1984. Persons and humans refashioning ourselves in a better image and likeness. *Zygon* 19:281–95.

Freedman, David Noel. 1987. Yahweh of Samaria and his Asherah. *Biblical Archaeologist* 50:241–49.

Glover, Jonathan. 1984. *What Sort of People Should There Be?* Middlesex, England: Penguin Books.

Gottwald, Norman K. 1979. *The Tribes of Yahweh: A Sociology of the Religion of Liberated Israel 1250–1050. B.C.E.* Maryknoll, N.Y.: Orbis Books.

Harrelson, Walter. 1969. *From Fertility Cult to Worship*. Garden City, N.Y.: Doubleday & Co.

Hopkins, David C. 1985. *The Highlands of Canaan*. Sheffield, England: Almond Press.

Howie, Carl G. 1982. Bio-ethics: A theological frontier. *Church & Society* 73:62–67.

Kenney, Martin, and Frederick Buttel. 1985. Biotechnology: prospects and dilemmas for Third World development. *Development and Change* 16:61–91.

Lebacqz, Karen, ed. 1983. *Genetics, Ethics and Parenthood*. New York: Pilgrim Press.

Ledley, Fred D. 1987. Somatic gene therapy for human disease: A problem of eugenics? *Trends in Genetics* 3:112–15.

Lewin, Roger. 1988a. Conflict over DNA clock results. *Science* 241:1598–1600.

―――. 1988b. Trees from genes and tongues. *Science* 242:514.

Mayr, Ernst. 1988. *Toward a New Philosophy of Biology: Observations of an Evolutionist*. Cambridge: Harvard University Press.

Mettinger, Tryggve N. D. 1988. [1987.] *In Search of God*. Trans. F. H. Cryer. Philadelphia: Fortress Press.

Moraczewski, Albert S., O.P., ed. 1983. *Genetic Medicine and Engineering: Ethical and Social Dimensions*. St. Louis: The Catholic Health Association of the United States.

Nebelsick, Harold P. 1987. God, creation, salvation and modern science. *Horizons in Biblical Theology* 9:79–103.

Patai, Raphael. 1967. *The Hebrew Goddess*. New York: Ktav Publishing House.

Patrides, C. A. 1966. *Milton and the Christian Tradition*. Oxford: Clarendon Press.

Peacocke, Arthur R. 1986. *God and the New Biology*. San Francisco: Harper & Row.

Peters, Ted. 1989. Cosmos as Creation. In *Cosmos as Creation: Theology and Science in Consonance*, ed. Ted Peters, pp. 45–113. Nashville: Abingdon Press.

Potter, Van Rensselaer. 1971. *Bioethics: Bridge to the Future*. Englewood Cliffs, N.J.: Prentice-Hall.

Rabino, Isaac. 1991. The impact of activist pressures on recombinant DNA research. *Science, Techology, & Human Values* 16:70–87.

Roberts, Leslie. 1988. Hard choices ahead for biodiversity. *Science* 241:1759–61.

Ruse, Michael. 1984. Genesis revisited: Can we do better than God? *Zygon* 19:297–316.

Schmitz, Philipp. 1989. An ethical look at agricultural biotechnology. Trans. D. Livingstone. In *Ethics in the Natural Sciences,* ed. Dietmar Mieth and Jacques Pohier (English language ed. P. Hillyer), pp. 127–37. Edinburgh: T. & T. Clark.

Schotsmans, Paul. 1989. *Brave New World* within reach? The genetic challenge to ethics. Trans. R. Nowell. In *Ethics in the Natural Sciences,* ed. Dietmar Mieth and Jacques Pohier (English language ed. P. Hillyer), pp. 89–104. Edinburgh: T. & T. Clark.

Sloan, Phillip R. 1985. The question of natural purpose. In *Evolution and Creation,* ed. Ernan McMullin, pp. 121–50. Notre Dame, Ind.: University of Notre Dame Press.

Strobel, Henry W. 1987. Recombinant DNA technology and the relationship of humanity to God: A plea for thought about the effects of developments in modern molecular biology on theological considerations. *St. Luke's Journal of Theology* 30:265–71.

Stubbe, Hans. 1972. [1965.] *History of Genetics: From Prehistoric Times to the Rediscovery of Mendel's Laws.* Trans. T. R. W. Waters. Cambridge, Mass.: MIT Press.

Theissen, Gerd. 1985. *Biblical Faith: An Evolutionary Approach.* Trans. J. Bowden. Philadelphia: Fortress Press.

Toulmin, Stephen. 1990. Theology in the context of the university. *Theological Education* 26:51–65.

Varga, Andrew C., S.J. 1985. "Playing God": The ethics of biotechnical intervention. *Thought* 60:181–95.

von Rad, Gerhard. 1961. *Genesis: A Commentary.* Trans. J. H. Marks. Philadelphia: Westminster Press.

Watson, James D. 1990. The Human Genome Project: Past, present, and future. *Science* 248:44–49.

Westermann, Claus. 1974. *Creation.* Trans. J. Scullion. Philadelphia: Fortress Press.

White, Lynn, Jr. 1967. On the historical roots of the ecological crisis. *Science* 155:1203–7.

Zimmerli, Walther. 1989. Is the technologisation of nature ethical? Trans. J. G. Cumming. In *Ethics in the Natural Sciences,* ed. Dietmar Mieth and Jacques Pohier (English language ed. P. Hillyer), pp. 138–1450. Edinburgh: T. & T. Clark.

Index

10 Cultural values being edited into genetic code   43   49   neutral → selective

38 → improve farming, → damage,
   unintended
44 reduced to matter   end we did not intend

48 Mesui - safe reflective distance

62 Purpose — how do we edit it into genetic code

61 men-gods do what they can do

67 to make a better human vs better environment

68 to suffer redemptively   . see 2ygon

   We are part of nature and yet stand apart

79 are we to correct genetic defects ? and
   thereby go "against" nature — what is natural

74 Justice issues
75 → feeding & healing ministry   cf 62
                ordered
86 Creation good but disordered

Co-creation   100, 114 (Hauveraus)

JUSTICE — can't wait for ethicists (R.C & Prot)
   to agree — sacrifice a few thousand
   embyros will a few million children
   and adult die